Praise for THE LONG RED THREAD

"Kyle Kondik has the rare ability to combine real-world mastery of politics with the erudition of political science research. In *The Long Red Thread*, he unspools a spritely and much-needed history of the last six decades of House elections as the chamber morphed from a safe and sleepy Democratic bastion to today's cauldron of hyper-nationalized politics."

—Walter Shapiro, staff writer at the *New Republic* and *Roll Call* columnist

"The *Long Red Thread* presents a detailed but concise account of the evolution of district-level voting patterns in congressional elections since 1964 that, among other things, deftly exposes the electoral roots of Congress's current susceptibility to stalemate and dysfunction. Anyone hoping to understand how American government arrived at its current unhappy state will find it illuminating."

—Gary C. Jacobson, author of *The Electoral Origins of Divided Government: Competition in U.S. House Elections, 1946–1988* and coauthor of *The Politics of Congressional Elections*

"In *The Long Red Thread*, Kyle Kondik provides an in-depth analysis of an important trend that has largely been ignored by scholars: the long-term shift in competition in US House elections that has given Republicans a narrow but significant advantage. This book is a must-read for scholars and students of contemporary American electoral politics."

—Alan I. Abramowitz, author of *The Great Alignment: Race, Party Transformation, and the Rise of Donald Trump*

"Kyle Kondik is one of the brightest young stars in the firmament of election analysis, and his new book, *The Long Red Thread*, proves that anew. Kondik shows how Democrats lost their twentieth-century advantage in the critical process of redistricting, leaving Republicans with yet another arrow in their quiver for control of American politics. Kyle's style, rich with colorful history and relevant detail, is sure to draw you in as he reveals some well-kept secrets of political power."

—Larry J. Sabato, founding director of the University of Virginia Center for Politics and editor in chief of *Sabato's Crystal Ball*

"Recounting more than a half-century of electoral history, Kyle Kondik documents how partisanship and electoral advantage can be amplified through reapportionment and redistricting practices. A crucially important story of how the House electoral map that once favored Democrats now tilts toward the GOP, *The Long Red Thread* is a must read for anyone seeking to understand the structures that affect electoral outcomes and determine our political futures."

—Douglas B. Harris, coauthor of *At War with Government: How Conservatives Weaponized Distrust from Goldwater to Trump*

THE LONG RED THREAD

THE LONG
RED THREAD

How Democratic Dominance Gave Way to
Republican Advantage in US House Elections

KYLE KONDIK

Foreword by Douglas B. Harris

OHIO UNIVERSITY PRESS ★ ATHENS

Ohio University Press, Athens, Ohio 45701
ohioswallow.com
© 2021 by Ohio University Press
All rights reserved

To obtain permission to quote, reprint, or otherwise reproduce
or distribute material from Ohio University Press publications,
please contact our rights and permissions department at
(740) 593-1154 or (740) 593-4536 (fax).

Cover design by Beth Pratt

Printed in the United States of America
Ohio University Press books are printed on acid-free paper ∞ ™

31 30 29 28 27 26 25 24 23 22 21   5 4 3 2 1

Library of Congress Cataloging-in-Publication Data
Names: Kondik, Kyle, author.
Title: The long red thread : how Democratic dominance gave way to Republican
advantage in US House elections / Kyle Kondik ; foreword by Douglas B. Harris.
Description: Athens : Ohio University Press, 2021. | Includes bibliographical refer-
ences and index.
Identifiers: LCCN 2021019577 (print) | LCCN 2021019578 (ebook) | ISBN
9780821424421 (paperback) | ISBN 9780821447345 (pdf)
Subjects: LCSH: United States. Congress. House—Election districts—History.
| United States. Congress. House—Elections. | Apportionment (Election law)—
United States—History. | United States—Politics and government—1945–1989. |
United States—Politics and government—1989–
Classification: LCC JK1341 .K66 2021 (print) | LCC JK1341 (ebook) | DDC
324.973/092—dc23
LC record available at https://lccn.loc.gov/2021019577
LC ebook record available at https://lccn.loc.gov/2021019578

To Lottie and Albie

CONTENTS

ILLUSTRATIONS

TABLES

FIGURES

FOREWORD

Over half a century ago, in a book called *The Real Majority: An Extraordinary Examination of the American Electorate,* Richard Scammon and Ben Wattenberg distinguished between "pebble watching" (a reference to the ancient Greek system of counting by pebbles, or *psephos,* in tabulating votes) and "tide watching" (the election watcher's practice of accounting not just for individual vote choice but also for the electorate as a whole and for the partisan patterns that emerged from the decisions it rendered).[1] To keep an eye on both the pebbles and the tides, election watchers, professionals, and rank amateurs alike, we must think in holistic ways that account for voters and the electorate, for parties and candidate campaigns, and for geography and the electoral maps that amplify some voters' voices at the relative expense of others.

It's worth pointing out that watching elections—the net gains of one party over the other in an election and over several succeeding elections—matters more for democratic governance than the sport and excitement they can provide. As is frequently uttered in contemporary political commentary, elections have consequences. Astute election watchers thus have something important to tell us about the broader political system, the law, and public policy. To understand America's policy future, one must understand its elections.

There are, to be sure, many books that watch the pebbles by tracking votes and opinions, but there are surprisingly few that keep an eye on the tides. But any quality election watcher knows that understanding elections and their outcomes demands attention to multiple elements—voters, candidates, campaigns, and formal legal district and state boundaries—that are essential to interpreting election outcomes. Moreover, these elements of elections are products themselves of a constitutional legal framework as well as of decisions made by governing institutions, including the

Supreme Court, which interprets the US Constitution and the law, the state legislatures that draw district lines, and even sometimes other institutions of government that shape the context in which election contests happen. To be sure, constitutional factors, such as the Senate's apportionment disparities or the Electoral College, are more obvious in their impact on other institutions' elections. But the House of Representatives, including its election outcomes and membership, is also a construct of the US Constitution and other institutional pressures that exist outside of its control. Indeed, not only are the Supreme Court and state legislatures critical actors in shaping the House, but the US Department of Justice, for example, also plays an important role in the story told in this book.

In *The Long Red Thread*, Kyle Kondik (himself a noted professional psephologist and tide watcher) tells the crucial history of how the House of Representatives electoral map went from tilting significantly in favor of the Democrats in the mid to late 20th century to having a (slightly less steep) tilt in favor of the GOP in the contemporary era. This is not to say that the Democrats cannot compete; they can, and they can win. Indeed, they won majorities in the recent 2018 and 2020 elections. Still, the Democrats compete at a disadvantage. The House electoral map favors Republicans. And just as election watchers should by now be well aware of the Republicans' "head start" in the Electoral College and the decided advantages they enjoy due to the Senate's apportionment magnifying the voice of those who live in less-populated (often Republican) states, the GOP has a clear advantage in the House as well. This is the crucial finding documented in this book.

In telling this important story, *The Long Red Thread* also documents several important trends and beneficially complements other important scholarly work that seeks to make sense of the contemporary electoral terrain.

First, the contemporary scholarship on parties and polarization has focused repeated attention on the partisan and geographic "sorting" of the electorate. In partisan terms, liberals and conservatives increasingly sort themselves into the Democratic and Republican parties, respectively. Of course, this was not always the case. In the mid-20th century, well after the New Deal had taken the national Democrats in a more leftward direction, some of the most conservative members of Congress hailed from the

South and still identified with the party of Thomas Jefferson and Jefferson Davis. But a partisan realignment, particularly but not exclusively a southern realignment, also led to a geographic sorting that made the South no longer the Democrats' "Solid South" but instead the Republican base. When this realignment is examined in historical detail from the 1960s to now, what is notable is how the Democrats maintained strength in southern congressional districts early on even as the GOP was nationalizing races and winning at the top of the ticket. The eventual upward trend of Republican victories in southern House seats since the late 1970s is unmistakable and has crucially changed American politics generally and the House of Representatives specifically.

Another variant of geographic sorting—the concentration of Democrats in cities and the strength of Republicans in rural areas, with the suburbs being increasingly crucial electoral battlegrounds—has had decided advantages for the GOP, particularly as apportionment questions and redistricting politics came to the foreground. The Reapportionment Revolution spurred by the Supreme Court's decisions in *Baker v. Carr* (1962) and *Wesberry v. Sanders* (1964) led, first, to the need to equalize districts in terms of population and then to politically consequential decisions of state legislatures to redraw district lines after the decennial census (usually to achieve an advantage for one of the two dominant parties). If both parties have won some redistricting battles, the fact that Republicans have proven more determined and successful than Democrats at drawing the lines on the map is a key part of this story. As Kondik demonstrates, one key consequence is the increasing alignment of electoral outcomes in House races and that district's presidential vote. The steep fall-off of "crossover" districts (districts that split their choice between the two parties in selecting the president and their House member) affects both our elections and the internal alignments within the House.

As for "the tides" that have come in and receded since the 1960s, they have increasingly favored the GOP. Sometimes, of course, the waves come in big, and sometimes they merely lap the shore. This book accounts for both big-wave elections, like 1974, 1994, 2010, or 2018, and those moments of stability in the House (such as what Kondik calls "Nixon's lonely landslide" in 1972) or when minimal gains seem to be canceled out over the course of successive elections, as was the case when Republicans picked up 16 seats during Ronald Reagan's 49-state landslide in 1984 (but suffered a net loss of 15 in the ensuing three elections). In chronicling these changes over time, Kondik carefully assesses the ways in which redistricting and reapportionment are drivers of both stasis and change. But he also wisely situates each election in its broader context, noting when a party's election wins are attributable (and when they are not attributable) to these districting factors.

This book's assessment of the cumulative effects of these tidal forces amounts to more than a half century of electoral history and, importantly, a keen understanding of the changing answer to this question: Which party does the map favor? Historically oriented election watchers are more prone to ask such questions when we look at the Electoral College map or the malapportionment in the Senate, but there is a similar story with regard to the House. At one time, the House electoral map tilted decidedly in the Democrats' favor. But when the Democrats held those majorities—some of which were quite large—significant internal divisions hampered their legislative effectiveness. But now the map works in favor of Republicans. And the Republican majorities, although smaller than the Democratic majorities of yesteryear, are far more unified than the Democrat majorities had been. One effect of electoral polarization and the decline of crossover districts is the increasing unity displayed within legislative parties. If the majority remains unified, even if relatively small or razor thin, that unity can stoke more legislative partisanship and further antagonize the minority. Yet the majority can still pass bills and, under the right conditions in the broader system, produce policy outcomes.

A third, crucially important, story that *The Long Red Thread* contributes to is our understanding of the 1994 Republican Revolution. In that election, the Newt Gingrich–led House GOP rode a wave of dissatisfaction with the Clinton administration and its "Contract with America" to capture the House majority party for the first time in 40 years. Breaking the Democrats' seeming lock on the House majority was a historic achievement that scholars have examined repeatedly. But most of those examinations generally focus on the story inside Congress—on how Gingrich's combativeness inside the House galvanized the House GOP, stoked interparty rivalries, and led to Republican control.

But the Gingrich effort was multifaceted, and his revolution was happening inside and outside the House. If, inside the House, Gingrich headed the "Conservative Opportunity Society" that was known for its polarizing politics in speech giving and combativeness with House Democratic leaders on the floor, he also was planning electoral strategy. As head of GOPAC, Gingrich led the effort to train and field Republican candidates throughout the country to take advantage of the electoral opportunities that new voter alignments *and new maps* were providing. *The Long Red Thread* tells an important and comparatively obscure part of this historic narrative—that the GOP's rise was as much a long-term electoral story based in congressional districts and elections taking place back home as it was a story that played out within the halls of Congress. For all the scholarly attention devoted to the historical "moment" that was the Republican Revolution, a key part of the story has been largely untold until now. The story of the Republican House majority that culminated in 1994 is a product of the Reapportionment Revolution begun 30 years before, and Kondik tells that part of the story as well as anyone.

Of course, this matters for current politics too. The general trend of Republican control of the House of Representatives that started in the 1990s is at least partly a product of the GOP's continued advantage in redistricting politics and the House electoral map. As with the Senate and (twice this century) the presidency, the Democrats can win the majority of votes nationally and still not win House control. And when the two parties are evenly divided, the advantage goes to Republicans—thanks to the map's tilt. This is a fact of electoral life in 21st-century American politics that conditions how Republicans campaign and govern and limits the extent to which demographic trends in the electorate favorable to the Democrats will result in seats, House control, and policy wins for them.

Finally, it is worth noting that the trends described in this book likely have consequences for the character of our leaders and the prospects for governing going forward. One of my stock lines in the classroom when discussing elections is "If we go to the map to see who won, it seems that the map won—again." The 21st century has seen many skilled politicians falter—a Republican in Maryland, a Democrat in Tennessee or Montana—not because they wouldn't make a good governor, senator, or

House member but because they lived in the wrong place. Good, capable Democratic candidates—however talented or tailor-made for a district—lose out to lesser lights in Republican terrain just as the GOP's most talented members fall hard when confronted with inhospitable geography when caught inside the wrong "lines on the map." An under-told story of contemporary politics is just how much "the map" wastes a lot of talent in this way. This is especially the case in the House, where lines are drawn specifically to accentuate partisan advantage.

Douglas B. Harris
Loyola University Maryland

PREFACE

While updating this book following the 2020 election, I came to a couple of conclusions.

The first was that the surprising results of 2020's House of Representatives elections, in which Democrats only narrowly held their majority in the House, made the arguments in the book stronger. While Democrats won more seats than Republicans, the party nearly lost its majority even as its presidential nominee, Joe Biden, won the election. This outcome helped illustrate the Democrats' perilous position in the House, a reversal of the dominant edge the party held in the chamber prior to the Republican takeover in 1994.

As someone who handicaps House elections, I also concluded that my projections in the last election could have been more accurate had I paid greater heed to some of the historical trends explored in this book. For one thing, if I had focused more on the declining power of incumbency and the increasing correlation between presidential and House results, I probably would have picked more Democratic incumbents to lose in districts that Donald Trump was likely to carry. Although, I was hardly alone in being thrown off by the House results in 2020. The electorate is still squirrelly enough to humble pundits on a regular basis.

This book is coming out in fall 2021, in the midst of the still-unfolding decennial redistricting process. With Republicans holding more power than Democrats in map drawing while also being in the advantageous position of not holding the presidency during a midterm election cycle, there were many reasons to believe that the Republicans would, in 2022, net the five seats they needed to flip control of the House after the Democrats won a 222–213 majority in 2020. It must be noted, though, that the last time a party had won such a narrow House majority was the Republicans in 2000, who had to defend a 222–213 edge in the first midterm of Republican president George W. Bush. Republicans ended up overcoming the usual White House midterm penalty, aided not only by redistricting but also by an unusual midterm environment colored by the aftermath of the devastating September 11 attacks and the lead-up to the Iraq War, which would begin in early 2003 after the 2002 midterm.

This is just a roundabout way of saying that while Republicans are well positioned to win back the House majority in 2022, events could intervene and upset that conventional wisdom. (I wouldn't be a political handicapper if I didn't include at least a few caveats.)

This project is an updated and expanded version of my master's thesis, which I defended in August 2019 as part of the master of arts in government program at Johns Hopkins University. What started as a project focused on redistricting evolved into a history of House elections since the early 1960s, when a series of landmark US Supreme Court decisions determined that both US House and state legislative districts had to have roughly equal population sizes. Portions of chapter 3 contain material adapted from my previously published work included in the postelection books I coedited with my colleagues at the University of Virginia Center for Politics and published by Rowman and Littlefield (full citations are listed in the bibliography).

This book is structured in three main chapters covering three important periods: 1964–74, a time of Democratic dominance in which states had to reckon with the reapportionment decisions; 1976–94, the lead-up to and culmination of the Republicans' efforts to capture the US House majority; and 1996–2020, an era of intense competition for House majorities in which Republicans have held power more often than Democrats. Each chapter is divided into two parts. The first part covers the academic literature related to the major themes of the chapter, while the second gives the granular details of each election year included in the chapter. Taken together, the book focuses on what I have found, as both a student at Johns Hopkins and as a congressional election analyst over the past decade, are the most important developments and trends in House elections since the 1960s.

Beyond showing the evolution of the House from unquestioned Democratic domination to arguable Republican advantage, this book seeks to provide something that is missing from the expansive universe of recent works on the House: a concise, single-volume history of US House elections from the so-called Reapportionment Revolution through the modern day. It blends the political science literature on House elections, which skews toward the quantitative, with analyses from sources such as the *Almanac of American Politics,* which provide an abundance of descriptive examples that add detail and context to the larger trends.

I'd like to thank everyone at Johns Hopkins who provided instruction and feedback on this project: Benjamin Ginsberg, Douglas Harris, Kathy Wagner Hill, Matt Laslo, Collin Paschall, Jacob Straus, Adam Wolfson, and Dorothea Wolfson. Harris deserves special thanks for also contributing an excellent foreword to this book. I also want to thank my dear friend Alex Beres, who helped persuade me to continue my formal education and went through the program with me. I'd also like to thank my colleagues at the University of Virginia Center for Politics, most notably Director Larry J. Sabato, Associate Director Kenneth Stroupe, Chief Financial Officer Mary Daniel Brown, and my fellow *Sabato's Crystal Ball* editor, J. Miles Coleman, who have all supported me over the years. I was also pleased that Ohio University Press was interested in once again publishing my work.

Any errors or omissions are my own.

Kyle Kondik
Washington, DC, June 2021

INTRODUCTION

From Dark Blue to Light Red

Four days before the 1994 election, President Bill Clinton heard a prediction from a top advisor that he didn't believe. Dick Morris, a Republican operative whom Clinton's staff found so distasteful that the president hid his relationship with him, told Clinton that Democrats were going to lose their majority in the US House of Representatives. "No way, no way," Clinton responded.[1]

Few could blame Clinton for being incredulous about Morris's prediction. Democratic control of the House had been a given for decades. Save for brief two-year majorities the Republicans won in 1946 and 1952, the Democrats had held the House uninterrupted since they took a majority in a series of special elections in 1931, allowing them to capture the gavel when the House opened that year in December.[2]

And yet Morris, of course, was right.

The Republican Revolution of 1994 represents a transitional point between more than a half century of Democratic dominance in the House and a more recent period that does not qualify as Republican "dominance" but is certainly more than just a slight political imbalance. In the years since 1994, Republicans will have held the House majority for 20 of the 28 years between 1995 and 2023, and they appear to hold more advantages in the race for majority control of the US House of Representatives than the Democrats. But these advantages are not unassailable. Already, the Democrats have won House majorities in 4 of the 13 elections since 1994, whereas the Republicans only won majorities in 2 elections between the New Deal and their 1994 breakthrough.

It may seem off base to argue that the nation is in the midst of a period of Republican advantage in the House while the Democrats currently hold a majority (albeit a reduced one following Democratic setbacks in the 2020 election). Yet there are a number of factors that argue in favor of looking at the House as an institution in which Republicans are generally better positioned to capture majorities than Democrats are.

Overall, there are three major trends over the course of the six decades of House elections covered in this book that transformed the House from a body dominated by Democrats to one in which Republicans enjoy an ongoing electoral advantage. Those trends are nationalization, realignment, and reapportionment, all of which are inextricably linked.

1. Nationalization: Over the course of the period studied here, House results became increasingly correlated with presidential results. In the 1960s and 1970s, which serve as the beginning point of this study, it was common for presidential elections to feature a tremendous amount of down-ballot ticket splitting. For instance, during this period more than a quarter of House districts, even in closely contested presidential elections, could for instance vote for a Democrat for president and a Republican for the House, or vice versa. More recently, there has been far less ticket splitting and more nationalization of results, which helps Republicans and hurts Democrats because of the Republicans' stronger influence over the redistricting process in the past couple of decades paired with, arguably, disparities in national population distribution that disadvantage Democrats. Additionally, some of the factors that helped sustain Democratic majorities—such as the ideological diversity of members and the advantage of incumbency—have eroded in recent years as elections have become more nationalized rather than localized.

2. Realignment: Over the last six decades, the American electorate has realigned its preferences. The South, historically the nation's most ideologically conservative region, nonetheless helped sustain Democratic control of the House even as the national Democratic Party was moving left. Over time, conservatives in the South started voting up and

down the ballot for members of the more conservative
the Republicans. Meanwhile, ideologically less conservative
the West Coast and Northeast, have moved toward the Democra.
the more moderate Midwest oscillating between the two parties. The,
overall realigning trends have generally benefited the Republicans in
aggregate.

3. Reapportionment: As noted above, Republicans over the past few de-
    cades have had more success dealing with reapportionment—a term that
    covers not just the reallocation of House seats after each census based on
    population but also the process of drawing up new districts. The shifting
    of seats based on population changes from the slower-growing North-
    east and Midwest to the faster-growing South and West helped Repub-
    licans at a crucial time, specifically in advance of the 2002 midterm, to
    maintain their House majority. Reapportionment may end up benefiting
    Republicans in advance of the 2022 midterm as well.

The emergence of a persistent Republican edge in the House has
come at a time when the differences between the two parties have become increasingly stark. As political scientist Sam Rosenfeld argued in
his recent history of the origins of polarization, "The two major American
political parties are now sorted quite clearly along ideological lines. The
most liberal Republican member of Congress has amassed a voting record
that is consistently to the right of the most conservative Democrat."[3]

With more ideologically consistent parties—almost all the liberals in
the Democratic Party, and almost all of the conservatives in the Republican Party—there are fewer opportunities for legislative compromises. This
was obvious from two of the biggest legislative fights in Congress over the
past dozen years: the struggle to pass the Affordable Care Act in 2009–10,
led by Democrats, and the struggle to do away with that same legislation,
led by Republicans, in 2017.

Republicans decided to play no role in the passage of the Affordable
Care Act (also known as "Obamacare"). Not only was it legislation that
Republicans generally did not support on its merits, but they also decided
they did not want to provide bipartisan cover for majority Democrats.
They arguably were rewarded, electorally, for their efforts: Obamacare

became law, but the backlash from it helped Republicans win back control of the House in 2010.

When Republicans tried to unwind Obamacare in 2017, Democrats—then in the minority themselves—not only disagreed with the Republicans' health-care plans, but they were also disincentivized to provide bipartisan cover to the majority Republicans. The Republicans pushed an Obamacare repeal through the House with great effort, but those efforts died in the Senate. Democrats ran heavily on health care in 2018 and retook the majority. Political scientist Frances Lee, in her history of competition for majorities in the House and Senate, described how both parties have come to believe, with great justification, that they can win majorities not by working with the majority party but by fighting it tooth and nail.[4] That sort of behavior also makes more sense when there's not much ideological overlap between the two parties, which is true now but wasn't necessarily true a few decades ago. "These developments," Rosenfeld wrote, "have helped to give contemporary politics the distinctive character of high-stakes warfare."[5] This is all an elaborate way of saying that perhaps the only way the parties can truly govern is when they have unified control of Washington—that is, if the parties can govern at all. It is important to note that the ideological cohesion of the parties has not necessarily made congressional majorities more effective at passing legislation, according to research by Lee along with political scientist James M. Curry.[6]

Still, the majority party in the House has always been important, and it may be more important in a time of hard partisanship, ideological cohesion, and little bipartisan cooperation. So if in fact the Republicans have an advantage in the race for the House—an advantage that doesn't guarantee them perpetual control of the House but gives them a better chance at control than the Democrats—that has important consequences for governing.

What follows is an exploration of how the House transitioned from a period of Democratic dominance to one of Republican advantage. This work is divided into three chapters, which together explore all 29 biennial national House elections held from 1964 through 2020: more than half a century of US electoral history. Clearly, this history cannot cover every single election: with 435 seats at stake every two years, this period features

12,615 individual elections, which would be impossible (and tedious) to cover in a single work. Instead, this book looks for larger trends and uses compelling individual results from each election to highlight them.

The starting point for this work, 1964, is not selected randomly. It was the first election after a series of monumental Supreme Court decisions that injected the principle of "one person, one vote" into the drawing of congressional and state legislative districts. Prior to these decisions, US House districts were not required to have equal populations within states. But over the course of the mid to late 1960s, states changed their district maps to comply with these rulings. So 1964, the start of the Reapportionment Revolution, seemed like a logical place to begin a study on modern US House elections.

The first chapter covers the elections held from 1964 to 1974 and traces the changing district lines forced by the Supreme Court's reapportionment decisions. This was a period of huge Democratic majorities, and the changing lines did not seem to significantly affect that dominance. However, one begins to see stirrings of modern trends in this period, as the previously moribund Republican Party in the conservative (but at the time heavily Democratic) South began to assert itself more fully. It also offers a primer and brief history of congressional redistricting.

The second chapter brings the narrative up to 1994, when the Republicans finally won the House majority. Going election by election, this chapter traces how Republicans, despite remaining in the minority throughout the late 1970s and 1980s, did make subtle gains and, perhaps more importantly, avoided major losses while holding the White House for the entire 1980s. As explored much more deeply in the chapter, midterm elections are typically the engines of change in the House, and the sitting president's party often suffers major losses in such elections. Democrats failed to make major gains in such elections under Republican presidents during this era and ended up losing major ground themselves in a 1994 midterm election under a Democratic president. While chapter 1 focuses on the fallout from the Supreme Court's reapportionment decisions, chapter 2 assesses how redistricting based on race, which was pushed by the President George H. W. Bush–era Justice Department, had an impact on partisan control of the House.

Chapter 3 brings the story up to the present and describes the elections from 1996 to 2020. This was a period of consistent but not absolute Republican control, which was bolstered by stronger Republican control of the levers of redistricting power in many states, particularly during the post-2010 census round of redistricting. This chapter looks most deeply at such partisan "gerrymandering"—the drawing of district lines for partisan benefit—although discussions of districting choices and the political power that shapes them are prominent throughout this work.

The research for this project encompasses much of the key literature concerning electoral nationalization, electoral patterns, reapportionment, redistricting, and other factors. There are not necessarily "schools of thought" in studying House elections, although there are disagreements about how decisive factors such as redistricting are in electoral outcomes. This work takes something of a middle view on the redistricting question: on the one hand, there is voluminous evidence cited throughout that partisan redistricting affects outcomes and is important; on the other, this book does not go so far as to say that partisan redistricting can always guarantee outcomes or that redistricting can necessarily lock one party into majority control of the House.

If such a lock on power were possible, it might be that this work would be finalized during a Republican majority in the House that persisted despite a national preference for Democratic House control in 2018 (and, to a lesser extent, in 2020). But the Democrats did in fact win the House majority in 2018 and then held it in 2020, albeit narrowly. That does not necessarily mean that the Democrats do not have certain handicaps in the biennial battle for the House, but those handicaps are not impossible to overcome.

Data, Definitions, and Methodology

This work is heavily reliant on the *Almanac of American Politics,* which has been published continuously every two years starting in 1971. It is the source of all election results and presidential election results by congressional district for chapters 2 and 3 and for parts of chapter 1. Various editions of the *Almanac* are also cited heavily throughout. For chapter 1, which covers some elections contested before the first publication of the *Almanac,* district election results are from the 1964–68 editions of *America Votes.* District-level presidential results are supplemented by an unpublished compilation by House expert Gary Jacobson as well as by calculations from Daily Kos Elections. National House popular vote totals and "crossover" House district tallies—districts that vote for different parties for president and for House in a given year—are from the Brookings Institution's Vital Statistics on Congress (https://www.brookings.edu/multi-chapter-report /vital-statistics-on-congress/) or were compiled by the author. Political scientists Theodore S. Arrington and Jonathan Rodden also helpfully provided their data on, respectively, the House national popular vote and the percentage of crossover districts held by each party over time.

Regional definitions are as follows:

Greater South: Alabama, Arkansas, Florida, Georgia, Kentucky, Louisiana, Mississippi, North Carolina, Oklahoma, South Carolina, Tennessee, Texas, Virginia, and West Virginia.

Interior West: Alaska, Arizona, Colorado, Idaho, Kansas, Montana, Nebraska, Nevada, New Mexico, North Dakota, South Dakota, Utah, and Wyoming.

Midwest: Illinois, Indiana, Iowa, Michigan, Minnesota, Missouri, Ohio, and Wisconsin.

Northeast: Connecticut, Delaware, Maine, Maryland, Massachusetts, New Hampshire, New Jersey, New York, Pennsylvania, Rhode Island, and Vermont.

West Coast: California, Hawaii, Oregon, and Washington.

These definitions are the same as those established by political scientist David Hopkins in his book *Red Fighting Blue,* which explores the nation's political divides by geography. While noting that "there are no consensus definitions of geographic regions in the United States,"[1] Hopkins's framework proposes five distinct areas. One key note about Hopkins's regions is that his definition adds Kentucky, Oklahoma, and West Virginia to the 11 states of the Old Confederacy to create a Greater South region. While other analysts may restrict the South to the traditional definition—just the 11 former Confederate states—including these three states as part of the Greater South is appropriate when assessing House results. This is especially true given that all three states had a strong Democratic House tradition in the decades preceding the Reapportionment Revolution, similar to the more traditionally recognized southern states, and because these states "can be viewed as culturally and politically southern," as Hopkins argued.[2] In more recent times, all three states have also become reliably Republican in presidential elections and in their House delegations, just like much of the rest of the South. In any event, when these five regional terms are used throughout, they adhere to the definitions laid out above except when otherwise noted.

Districts are denoted using a state's postal abbreviation followed by the district number, which is a common way of denoting congressional districts in election analyses. So, "Rep. Abigail Spanberger (D, VA-7)" means that Spanberger is a Democrat who represents Virginia's Seventh Congressional District.

Calculations in the text are by the author unless otherwise cited. This includes the makeup of the House after each November election. Independents are counted as members of the party with whom they caucused or with whom they sought to caucus. So, as an example, then representative

Bernie Sanders (I, VT-AL) is counted as a Democrat in the elections in which he was elected (1990–2004) for the purposes of the overall tallies reported throughout this project, even though Sanders did not immediately become a member of the Democratic caucus when first elected.[3] Consequently, when Sanders left the House and was elected to the Senate in 2006, he was replaced by an actual Democrat, Rep. Peter Welch (D, VT-AL). This change is not reflected as a Democratic pickup in these calculations; instead it is treated as retained Democratic control of the seat. Throughout the period studied, there were only a few House members elected as neither Democrats nor Republicans, and these members who did not belong to one of the two major parties were never important in determining majority control—as opposed to, for instance, the House following the 1916 election, when Republicans won slightly more seats than Democrats. But support from members who did not belong to either of the two major parties allowed the Democrats to organize the House and elect a Democratic speaker.[4]

Additionally, the net change in seats from one election to the next is measured by comparing the House elected in one general election with that elected in the next election. For instance, it was commonly reported that the Democrats picked up 40 net seats in the 2018 election. That was true because the Democrats technically held 195 seats immediately going into that election (including a couple of vacant Democratic seats that were filled via special election in the November general election), and they won 235, a net gain of 40. However, Democrats only won 194 seats in the 2016 election. They won their 195th seat in a March 2018 special election. For the purposes of consistency across years, this book just reflects general election results from each even-numbered November election to the next. So because Democrats won 41 more House seats in 2018 than they won in 2016, their net gain is reported as 41, not 40.

ONE

The Partisan Consequences of the Reapportionment Revolution in the United States House of Representatives, 1964–74

The *New York Times* editorial board, writing in 1965, identified "twin evils" in drawing legislative districts: "malapportionment and gerrymandering."[1] Both feature prominently in the history of drawing US House districts. By the mid-1960s, the US Supreme Court had eliminated the former (malapportionment) yet has remained on the sidelines when it comes to the latter (partisan gerrymandering).

It may seem obvious that US House districts should have equal or at least roughly equal populations, but for most of American history that was not a stringent requirement. As political scientist Erik Engstrom wrote in his history of partisan gerrymandering, "Congress occasionally added provisions to various apportionment acts mandating that district populations be as equal as possible, but there is little evidence that these provisions were ever enforced, much less achieved."[2] As a result, House districts within states would often vary wildly in population size, creating "glaring disparities in voting power."[3] This was malapportionment.

Political scientist Andrew Hacker, writing in the midst of the legal battles that would lead to population equality in districts, found that of "the 42 states with more than one congressional district after the 1960 Census, exactly half contain[ed] constituencies where the vote of a citizen in the smallest congressional district [was] worth at least twice that of the citizen in the largest district."[4] For example, after the 1960 census Michigan had one congressional district with 802,994 residents while another had 177,431. According to Hacker, Michigan, along with Texas, was the most malapportioned state.[5]

The term *gerrymandering* arose from what may be the most famous political cartoon in American history, which depicted a legislative district shaped like a salamander. In 1812 the Democratic-Republican-controlled Massachusetts state legislature tried to maximize its number of seats in a new districting plan and minimize those held by the minority Federalists. Elbridge Gerry (pronounced with a hard *g*, like *Gary*), the Democratic-Republican governor, "disliked the plan but signed the remap into law anyway—a veto, he thought, would be improper."[6]

A Federalist newspaper cartoonist seized on a long, thin district that snaked from southwest to northeast, making an inverse *L*, and dubbed it the "gerry-mander," complete with wings, claws, and a snarling lizard's head. Thus emerged the gerrymander (pronounced in modern times with a soft *g*, like *Jerry*). Interestingly, the famous gerrymandered salamander district did not perform as intended, as the Federalists retook the district in the following year's elections.[7]

But this was not even the first partisan gerrymander. In an early study of gerrymanders, doctoral student Elmer Griffith found examples in the precolonial period.[8] Nor was it the first gerrymander that failed: James Madison, the father of the Constitution and a future president, faced a gerrymandered district in a contest against future president James Monroe, which Madison nonetheless won anyway.[9] From the very beginnings of gerrymandering, one can sense a theme: even if districts are nefariously drawn to benefit one party or candidate over the other, they do not always work out the way they are designed, whether in the district's initial election or in subsequent contests.

Throughout American history there has rarely been a consistent rhythm to congressional redistricting. Instead of the predictable pattern Americans have become accustomed to in recent decades—all states with more than one district draw new districts leading up to election years that end in a two in response to the release of a new census at the start of a decade—redistricting happened very often, or not often at all, depending on the state and the era.

Frequent redistricting was a prominent feature of late 19th-century politics, according to Engstrom: "In every year from 1862 and 1896, with one exception, at least one state redrew its congressional district boundaries. Ohio, for example, redrew its congressional district boundaries six times between 1878 and 1890."[10] The consequences of these remaps could be profound, such as in 1888 when Pennsylvania Republicans "engineered a last-minute redistricting that helped ensure a narrow Republican majority in the House."[11]

Redistricting became less common in the 20th century, and unchanging districts became "silent gerrymanders" that preserved party strength in many states through malapportionment.[12] Ohio, for instance, did not change its maps at all from 1914 to 1952, opting for stability over the wild gyrations it experienced in the late 1800s.[13] Thus, malapportionment was used at times as a form of partisan gerrymandering. This became particularly pronounced in the decades leading up to the Supreme Court's reapportionment decisions.

One can see how failing to redistrict for decades could lead to population disparities between districts, particularly in a time when the urban population was growing much faster than the rural population. The explosion of the nation's urban population was a major reason for the rampant malapportionment that eventually pushed the Supreme Court to intervene and enshrine the concept of "one person, one vote" in congressional districting.

Many members of Congress, particularly those from rural districts, were spooked by the 1920 census, which reported that for the first time in American history a majority of the nation's population lived in urban as opposed to rural areas. "Not coincidentally," wrote historian J. Douglas Smith in his history of the Supreme Court's reapportionment decisions, "Congress that year failed to reapportion the House of Representatives for the first—and, as it turned out, only—time in American history." When Congress finally got around to passing the Reapportionment Act of 1929, it "freed states to draw congressional districts that were neither compact nor contiguous, and that made no pretense of containing equal numbers of inhabitants."[14] Engstrom found that district lines in many states were not revised with population changes and that the average population deviation between districts within states rose in the 20th century.[15]

While the debate over malapportionment typically focused on cities versus rural areas, Smith wrote, suburban areas were the places that were really exploding in population in the middle of the 20th century—between 1950 and 1960, the population in many of the nation's central cities started to fall while populations rose dramatically in surrounding suburban areas.[16] These growing suburbs stood a lot to gain in terms of political representation if malapportionment ended.

The US Supreme Court, long operating outside of what conservative justice Felix Frankfurter called the "political thicket"[17] of congressional redistricting and reapportionment, decided in *Baker v. Carr* (1962) that it could intervene in such cases. Two years later, the Supreme Court decided in *Wesberry v. Sanders* (1964) that "as nearly as is practicable, one person's vote in a congressional election is to be worth as much as another's."[18] The *Wesberry* decision forced states to redraw their districts to address malapportionment. Change happened quickly: every state adopted new congressional districts to comply with the ruling by 1967, just a few years after the landmark *Wesberry* ruling.[19] This was the Reapportionment Revolution, and over time, states have found it increasingly difficult to justify, and courts have been increasingly reluctant to grant, any deviations from absolute equality in congressional district size, redistricting expert Charles S. Bullock III writes.[20] In 2002, for instance, a federal court struck down a Pennsylvania map that had a population range of just 19 people.[21]

Wesberry pushed states to redraw their congressional districts, forcing the creation of new maps to equalize populations among districts and then regular redistricting in response to the population changes indicated by the decennial census. Since *Wesberry* all states have fallen into a routine in which they draw new maps to account for population changes every 10 years. However, on occasion states or courts redraw districts in the middle of a decade, for example, when Republican lawmakers in Texas replaced a Democrat-friendly map with their own after their party won control of the state legislature in 2002. Some states forbid such power plays: the Colorado Supreme Court blocked a middecade redistricting effort by the

Republican-controlled legislature in 2003, determining that the state's constitution allowed only a single round of congressional redistricting following each decennial census.[22] There remain no federal prohibitions on frequent redistricting.

In *Wesberry*'s wake, some observers felt that the court's decision would prompt more partisan gerrymandering.[23] That's not to say gerrymandering did not happen in the decades before *Wesberry*. For instance, political scientist David Mayhew found that "ingenious cartographic efforts" in California and New York prior to the 1952 election may have been decisive in helping Republicans win a national House majority that year,[24] which was one of only two times Republicans won the House over a six-decade span from the early 1930s to the early 1990s. But according to political scientists Nathaniel Persily, Thad Kousser, and Patrick Egan, *Wesberry* may have opened the door to such gerrymandering becoming more common: "Although it is true that before 1962, parties in control of legislatures could target their opponents for elimination, the practice became routinized once the Court mandated decennial redistricting."[25] Political scientist Robert J. Sickels argued in the aftermath of the reapportionment decisions that "court-ordered redistricting was viewed as an invitation to compensate for the loss of one tool of gerrymandering by the sharpening of others."[26] In other words, Sickels suggested that the Reapportionment Revolution served as a prompt for states to gerrymander.

Overall, though, political scientists tended to downplay the importance of partisan gerrymandering in the immediate aftermath of the Reapportionment Revolution. Writing in 1972, political scientist Robert Erikson observed that "partisan control of the districting scheme is not as important a determinant of partisan control of the state's congressional districts as might be thought."[27]

While the court did away with malapportionment, it has not limited partisan gerrymandering. The Supreme Court has never imposed practical standards on the practice. In 2004's *Vieth v. Jubelirer* decision, a five-to-four majority (led by then swing justice Anthony Kennedy), determined there was no way for the court to determine what was (or was not) an impermissible partisan gerrymander.[28] In 2019's *Rucho v. Common Cause*, Chief Justice John Roberts, writing for a five-to-four majority once again on this issue, determined that "partisan gerrymandering claims present political questions beyond the reach of the federal courts."[29] So although the court once decided to enter the political thicket of population equality, it has resisted entering the thicket of partisan redistricting.

At the dawn of the post–Reapportionment Revolution era, congressional line drawers found themselves constrained by district population size but little else. What follows is an examination of the immediate partisan consequences of the Reapportionment Revolution, from the implementation of the new maps through the pivotal 1974 midterm election, in which Democrats made significant gains in the House in the aftermath of the Watergate scandal and President Richard Nixon's resignation. The era studied is bookended by two elections, 1964 and 1974, which featured some of the strongest electoral performances in the history of the Democratic Party. In 1964, Democrats captured 295 House seats and took 291 in 1974.

So while there was not a direct, short-term impact on the Democrats' dominance in the House, the individual seats that made up those big Democratic majorities did change on a state-by-state level, and those changing patterns in the post-*Wesberry* world provided some clues about the future shape of the House.

AFTER THE REAPPORTIONMENT REVOLUTION

The end of malapportionment may have benefited Democrats, at least outside the party's then preserve in the South. A persistent pro-Republican bias in nonsouthern House results disappeared in the mid to late 1960s and "can be explained largely by the changing composition of northern districting plans," political scientists Gary Cox and Jonathan Katz found.[30] The Democrats won better maps in the North in part because they found themselves in a strong partisan position heading into redistricting and because a majority of the nonsouthern House maps at the state level were either drawn by Republicans or were modifications of previous Republican-drawn plans.[31] Overall, political scientist Ward Elliott argued that the "Reapportionment Revolution took place at a particularly bad time for the Republicans; namely, after the elections of 1964,"[32] when Republicans had lost hundreds of state legislative seats nationally thanks to President Lyndon B. Johnson's (D) strong national victory, leaving Republicans with a weak hand to play as most states redrew their maps to comply with *Wesberry* following that election.

In the South, Democrats maintained a strong hold even after reapportionment, although this era did see southern Republicanism grow in strength. Immediately following World War II, there were only two Republicans in the entire 105-member House delegation covering the typically Democratic 11 states of the Civil War–era Confederacy.[33] "Beginning in the 1950s, however, the GOP started to register gains, which increased markedly in the 1960s," political scientist Seth McKee found in his study of the rise of the GOP in the southern US House delegation.[34] In the midst of the Reapportionment Revolution, the 1965 federal Voting Rights Act gave southern Blacks the franchise after it had been effectively denied them in many places by Jim Crow laws—introducing a new bloc of voters into the region and shaking up these states' moderate-to-conservative Democratic primary electorates. Black voters would begin to make their presence felt in southern House races in the late 1960s and early 1970s, playing a role in making Democratic primary electorates less conservative and helping to push southern conservatives toward the Republicans in the decades that followed, according to political scientist David Lublin.[35]

Eventually, the South would realign with the more conservative party, the Republican, both at the presidential and congressional level. Throughout the postwar era, party identification among southern Whites gradually became more Republican and less Democratic, but Republican identification only overtook Democratic identification in the 1990s, around the time of the decisive 1994 election, in which Republicans made major gains in the South, realizing their potential in this historically conservative region.[36] Redistricting was certainly a critical force in the lead-up to 1994, but how districts were historically drawn was not thought to affect that relationship in the 1960s, when the South's Democratic dominance was taken as a fact of life,[37] notes McKee, as evidenced by the Democrats' lopsided control of the region's House delegation at the time. Aggressive Democratic gerrymandering in southern states, most notably Texas, helped the party hang on to House seats that it otherwise might have lost in the late 20th century.

This southern dominance of the Democratic House delegation leads to an important point about 20th-century Democratic House majorities: ideologically, they were much different than the Democratic House majorities one might expect in the 21st century, and liberal influence waxed and waned as conservative southern Democrats and liberal northern Democrats often tried to coexist within the same long-running US House majority.

While Democrats ruled the House for an almost-unbroken six decades, from the New Deal through the early 1990s, conservatives still often held sway, and it's reasonable to view some elections as tilting the balance of power in the House even as the majority party, the Democrats, did not change.

For instance, Democrats lost 72 seats in the 1938 midterm. While Democrats still held a sizable majority—Republicans had only won a pitiful 89 seats in 1936, Franklin Roosevelt's landslide first reelection—the results of the 1938 election empowered the so-called conservative coalition, an alliance of conservative (mostly southern) Democrats and Republicans that "could usually be relied upon . . . [to impede] liberal interventionist policies at home and abroad," wrote political scientist Nicol Rae. This coalition had a "firm hold" on the House for 20 years after 1938, until dulled by the 1958 Democratic wave.[38] Mark C. Shelley II's study of the conservative coalition, *The Permanent Majority*, found that when the coalition formed on a particular vote, it won two-thirds of the roll-call votes in the House from 1933 to 1980. One period when the coalition struggled, though, was in 1965–66, when a huge liberal Democratic majority was able to push through President Lyndon B. Johnson's Great Society programs.[39] But after Republican gains in 1966, the coalition was empowered—again, even as Democrats retained the House.

This is a study primarily of election results, not governance. But the power of the conservative coalition during Democratic control of the House for much of the 20th century means that some of the elections in the period covered in this book, like 1966 and 1980 (in favor of conservatives) and 1964 and 1982 (in favor of liberals), had a significant impact on who was able to exercise power in the House, even as the majority party remained the same in all of those elections.

One other key factor for contemporary observers to remember is that the 1960s, 1970s, and 1980s featured a considerable amount of ticket splitting, with Republicans building an advantage in presidential contests but Democrats retaining a strong hold over the US House. For instance, in both the 1968 and 1976 presidential elections (two races decided by very narrow margins nationally), roughly 30 percent of House districts in both elections voted for different parties for president and for the House. In 2012, 2016, and 2020, less than 10 percent of all districts featured such a split. Who were the voters splitting their tickets? In general, there is no consensus on why ticket splitting occurred so regularly in that earlier period. "In some accounts," political scientist David Hopkins writes, "they were mostly middle-class professionals alienated by the [Democrats'] tolerance of high taxes and crime rates, while other descriptions portrayed them as largely consisting of white Catholics and blue-collar southerners dissatisfied with Democratic leaders' cultural permissiveness and dovish approach to foreign policy."[40]

Now let's move on to an analysis of the elections immediately following the Reapportionment Revolution.

1964: The House at the Dawn of the Reapportionment Revolution

House elected: 295–140 Democratic
Change from previous election: +36 Democratic

Nine months after the Supreme Court issued the *Wesberry* ruling, President Lyndon B. Johnson (D) won the largest share of the national popular vote (61.1 percent) of any presidential candidate of either party in the history of the modern two-party, Democrats-versus-Republicans era (since 1856).

Johnson's electoral coattails helped Democrats add 36 net seats to their already-large House majority, pushing the Democratic caucus to 295 members, a height the party had not reached since Franklin Roosevelt's New Deal (and a majority the size of which has not been matched by either party since). But the net gain for Democrats obscured some notable shifts in favor of the Republicans in the South.

Even though the Supreme Court handed down the *Wesberry* verdict in advance of the 1964 election, only five states immediately drew new maps in time for that election, meaning that most of the districts in place for 1964 were unaffected by the ruling.[41] Some of the districts that remained unchanged had been drawn in 1962 before *Wesberry*, but others had not been changed in decades.

Democrats captured 47 previously Republican seats in 1964 spread over 19 states. Almost a quarter of those gains (11) came in just two states— New Jersey (4) and New York (7)—and about a third (17) came from the Midwest, led by a 5-seat gain in Iowa and 4 seats apiece in Michigan and Ohio. Of these states featuring large Democratic gains, only Michigan drew new districts in advance of the 1964 election. Michigan also was the most malapportioned state in the country prior to the *Wesberry* ruling and merits a closer look.

Republicans controlled redistricting in Michigan both before and after *Wesberry*. But when a federal court invalidated the state's districts as noncompliant with *Wesberry* in March 1964, Republicans had little time to draw a new map before the November elections. The court told the state that if it did not draw a new map, the state would elect all of its members in statewide at-large elections, something Republicans did not want. That, plus a legislative time limit that Republicans lacked a two-thirds legislative majority to bypass, meant they had to make concessions to Democrats in the new map.[42]

Michigan's malapportionment did not necessarily come from a dramatic underrepresentation of big urban areas. Wayne County, home of Detroit, had six congressional districts both before and after the end of malapportionment, although there was a wide disparity among the populations of the six Wayne County districts that redistricting corrected. In any event, Wayne County sent six Democrats to the House both before and after *Wesberry*. Outside of Wayne County, the largest district by population was MI-18, which before redistricting covered all of Oakland County, encompassing some of the Detroit suburbs. It had about 690,000 residents. The smallest district by population, with about 177,000 residents, was MI-12, which covered the western half of the sparsely populated Upper Peninsula. Redistricting corrected these population imbalances by splitting Oakland County into two districts while combining the two districts that previously covered the Upper Peninsula and the state's northern tip.

Redistricting also gave Macomb County, another part of Greater Detroit, its own district. As noted earlier, growing suburban representation would be a prominent feature of many moves to correct malapportionment because these areas often were dramatically underrepresented in the House and accounted for a large share of population growth in the 1960s.[43] Additionally, a district that covered Flint and Lansing, the state capital, was split in two separate districts centered on each city. The state also eliminated a statewide at-large district it had created when the state received an extra seat following the 1960 census. Democrats performed well on the new map in the short term, netting four seats and flipping the state delegation from 11–8 Republican to 12–7 Democratic.

Republicans made gains of their own, though. The 1964 presidential election represented a sea change in American presidential elections as Republican nominee Barry Goldwater, running as an opponent of federal civil rights legislation, became the first Republican to ever carry all five states of the Deep South (Alabama, Georgia, Louisiana, Mississippi, and South Carolina). Goldwater won only one other state: his home state of Arizona. Unlike in the nation's other four regions, where Democrats netted 40 House seats overall, Republicans netted 4 House seats in the Greater South, fueled by Alabama, a state that also drew new House districts in 1964.

In 1962 statewide at-large elections, Alabama elected eight Democrats and no Republicans. It had lost a seat after the 1960 census and held statewide House elections instead of drawing new districts. The state did redistrict in 1964, although the districts it drew in some instances did not have the population equity required by *Wesberry*, thus forcing another redraw in 1966 that only impacted three districts.[44] After the 1964 redistricting, Republicans won five of eight House seats in Alabama despite fielding candidates in only six of the eight districts, so only one opposed Democrat actually won. Republican challengers won one open seat and defeated four Democratic incumbents, powered by Goldwater's nearly 70 percent statewide majority. This represented a lasting shift in Alabama. While Democrats would regain some of their lost ground in subsequent elections, Alabama did not have a single Republican House member prior to 1964. After 1964, it has never elected fewer than two in any election.

Georgia elected its first Republican House member since Reconstruction when Bo Callaway (R) won an open seat in GA-3, a rural district containing the city of Columbus in west-central Georgia. Goldwater's huge victory is likely the biggest reason Callaway won. Although redistricting changed the political landscape here in some respects—James P. Wesberry Jr., the namesake of the landmark Supreme Court case, was a Georgia resident, and the case immediately forced redistricting in that state—Goldwater easily carried every county in both the old and new versions of the district. Goldwater won the new GA-3 with 63 percent of the two-party vote; the old district had given just 33 percent of the two-party vote to Richard Nixon (R) four years earlier, a 30-point Republican swing that mirrored Georgia's state-level swing from Nixon to Goldwater.

Another southern gain came in Mississippi, where Prentiss Walker (R) defeated 22-year incumbent W. Arthur Winstead (D), who was the only Democrat unlucky enough to have a Republican opponent in 1964.[45] Had Republicans put up candidates in the other four districts, they likely would have picked up more seats in Mississippi that year, if its neighbor Alabama was any indication. A lack of candidates almost certainly cost Republicans elsewhere in the South: in the five Goldwater-won states, Republicans only ran candidates in 15 of 37 districts. Of those 15, 7 won—an impressive winning percentage in a region where Republicans hardly registered prior to Goldwater.

The House election in 1964 was something of a rarity for this era in that Democrats actually won a majority of nonsouthern House seats. That would not be the case two years later, even as Democrats lost additional ground in Dixie.

1966: REDISTRICTING BEGINS IN EARNEST AS REPUBLICANS STRIKE BACK

House elected: 248–187 Democratic
Change from previous election: +47 Republican

Midterm elections often break against the president's party, as political scientist Andrew Busch explains in his history of such elections: "The midterm election pattern virtually guarantees that the president's party will be hurt at regular intervals. The extent of that damage may vary considerably, but the fact of it rarely does."[46] There have been 40 midterm elections since the Civil War, and the president's party has lost ground in the House in 37 of those. The average loss is about 33 seats. Table 1.1 shows the net change in the House in midterm years from the end of World War II through 2018. As the table confirms, the president's party almost always loses seats, although the average seat loss since World War II is somewhat smaller, at 27.

Some election outcomes are worse than others for the presidential party—for instance, Democrats lost only four net seats in John F. Kennedy's lone midterm in 1962, the election immediately before the beginning of this study's timeframe—but 1966 held to the more traditional pattern, as Democrats lost 47 seats. Part of this was because the public was beginning to turn against Johnson thanks to public exasperation over his liberal Great Society programs and his handling of the war in Vietnam.[47] Another factor was simply that Democrats did not have anywhere to go but down from the huge House majority they won in 1964.

Table 1.1. Midterm House losses for presidential party, 1946–2018

Year	Party holding presidency	President's party gain/ loss of seats in House
1946	D	–55
1950	D	–29
1954	R	–18
1958	R	–48
1962	D	–4
1966	D	–47
1970	R	–12
1974	R	–48
1978	D	–15
1982	R	–26
1986	R	–5
1990	R	–8
1994	D	–54
1998	D	4
2002	R	7
2006	R	–30
2010	D	–64
2014	D	–13
2018	R	–41

Source: Compiled by author

Roughly half of the Republican gains came simply from retaking districts that had voted Democratic in 1964. Some of these districts probably did not have much business electing Democrats anyway, but they did in 1964 during a huge Democratic wave. For instance, in 1966 Democrats could not hold districts in traditionally Republican states like Nebraska, North Dakota, and Wyoming that they had captured somewhat surprisingly two years earlier. Iowa, which had given Democrats five net seats in 1964, turned four of them back red in 1966. Redistricting had nothing to do with these changes because none of these states drew new maps in response to *Wesberry* prior to the 1966 elections.

But redistricting may have made a difference elsewhere. Republicans gained 10 seats total from just two states in 1966, the aforementioned Michigan and its southern neighbor, Ohio. Both states had drawn new districts in this era—Michigan before 1964 and Ohio before 1966—and these changes likely affected their partisan balance.

Even though Democrats had seemingly benefited from the Michigan remap, the new map was not necessarily Democratic-leaning even though it produced a 12–7 Democratic delegation in 1964. Based on the two-party presidential vote, the state's median House seat was about two points to the right of the state—Johnson had won 67 percent statewide but only 65 percent in the median seat—and several of the Democratic gains were by small vote shares in 1964. With the changing political tides in 1966, and the Republicans holding a bit of an advantage on the map, Republicans were able to win back what they had lost in Michigan—and then some.

Ohio, too, saw Republicans claw back their 1964 losses. Democrats netted four seats in 1964 by less than five points apiece, and all four of those new Democratic incumbents lost in 1966's less favorable environment. The state also redistricted in between the two elections, and Republicans controlled the process. Three of the four new Democratic incumbents saw their districts substantially redrawn. Republicans also converted a statewide at-large seat into a favorable Republican-leaning seat in western Franklin County (Columbus). Franklin County needed a second seat to account for its growing population anyway—another example of an underrepresented suburban area—and back in the 1960s the county was very Republican (it would become very Democratic by the 2010s). The combination of 1966's

Republican-leaning political conditions coupled with a GOP-drawn map had disastrous consequences for Democrats in Ohio.

Republicanism in the South endured breakthroughs and setbacks in 1966. On one hand, Democrats recaptured two of the five seats they lost in Alabama two years prior, and they also won back their lost seat in Mississippi after Walker unsuccessfully ran for US Senate. On the other hand, Arkansas elected its first post-Reconstruction Republican in 1966, John Paul Hammerschmidt (R), after it redrew its districts. Hammerschmidt defeated a 22-year incumbent in James Trimble (D, AR-3). It's hard to say anything conclusive about the possible effect redistricting may have had on Hammerschmidt's win, but AR-3 was the most sparsely populated district in the state prior to redistricting, and thus it had to take on more territory. The district, which covered much of western Arkansas and included much of the then-Democratic state's ancestral Republican territory, picked up additional counties to the south of it, some of which had voted for Nixon in 1960 and thus probably made the district marginally more Republican. Redistricting in Florida created a new district in southern Florida, giving then-Republican-leaning Broward County (Fort Lauderdale) its own congressional district, which turned out to be an easy Republican pickup. This was not a historic breakthrough for Republicans in this southern state, however—they had already held two seats in the state prior to 1966.

While history-making Republican Callaway gave up his seat in Georgia to run unsuccessfully for governor, helping Democrats win back the seat, Republicans captured both of the seats in the Atlanta area, the underrepresentation of which spawned the *Wesberry* lawsuit. Wesberry himself was a resident of the old Atlanta-based GA-5, which prior to the court decision bearing his name had nearly three times the population of Georgia's least-populated district. Georgia's new districts did not lead to Republican gains in 1964—remember, the one seat the Republicans gained probably had little to do with redistricting—but the new plan did create an extra seat in the Atlanta area.

Other Republican gains south of the Mason-Dixon line came in Maryland, where redistricting turned a statewide at-large seat into a new seat centered on Montgomery County, which comprises some of the Washington,

DC, suburbs, and Tennessee, where new districts gave Memphis an additional representative. Republicans won four of nine seats in Tennessee that year, adding a Memphis seat to three the party already held in eastern Tennessee, which has been Republican for generations and opposed secession in the Civil War era.

In Virginia, the Old Dominion's new House map had to adjust for a growing population in northern Virginia, also in the DC suburbs. The new plan modified VA-8, home to powerful House Rules Committee chairman Howard Smith, a conservative Democrat who would lose a primary to a liberal challenger. A Republican then won the seat in the fall.

In Texas, a new redistricting plan boosted the representation of previously underrepresented big cities like Dallas and Houston. Future president George H. W. Bush (R) won a new Houston-area seat in 1966, part of two Republican victories in Texas that broke up the 23–0 House monopoly Democrats had won in Texas in 1964.

Republicans also added a seat in South Carolina in advance of the 1966 election not because of redistricting or by beating a Democrat but rather because segregationist Albert Watson switched parties following the 1964 election. Watson followed the lead of Sen. Strom Thurmond, who had switched from Democrat to Republican before the 1964 election. Watson resigned from Congress after the Democratic caucus stripped him of his seniority for backing Goldwater, and he ran in and won a special election for his old seat.[48]

Watson was the first of 15 conservative and mostly southern Democratic House members who would abandon the party from 1965 to the end of the century, according to a count from political scientists Timothy P. Nokken and Keith T. Poole's study of congressional party switchers.[49] Most of those came after Ronald Reagan's election as president in 1980.

As shown through some of these examples from 1966, the growing voting power of suburban areas forced by *Wesberry* likely benefited Republicans in the South in part because early southern Republicanism first emerged in big metropolitan areas in the first half of the 20th century. "Retirees from the Midwest and Northeast had begun to settle in Florida before the Depression, and the rise of Southern industry in the postwar South brought in Northern managers. They brought their Republican voting habits with them," writes political analyst Sean Trende.[50] George H. W. Bush himself is a good example of this trend—he was born in Massachusetts and then made his way to Texas, and his father was a senator from Connecticut. Overall, "the Supreme Court's reapportionment decisions had empowered Republicans voters in the suburbs every bit as much as they had Democrats in the shrinking cities," Smith writes.[51]

Republicans would lose some of these newfound southern urban and suburban seats in subsequent elections, when the national pendulum swung to the Democrats. But in a region known for Democratic dominance, Republican victories in the South—once unthinkable—were beginning to happen with more regularity, and the *Wesberry* decision likely contributed to some of these wins.

All told, Republicans captured a narrow 158–153 advantage in the non-southern United States in the 1966 House elections. But Democrats easily maintained the overall majority thanks to a 95–29 edge in the 14 states of the Greater South.

1968–70: Years of Stasis

House elected (1968): 243–192 Democratic
Change from previous election: +5 Republican
House elected (1970): 255–180 Democratic
Change from previous election: +12 Democratic

House maps remained in flux after the 1966 election, as 17 states redrew again in advance of the 1968 election. That election took place in the shadow of the concurrent Vietnam War; the decision of President Johnson not to seek reelection; the assassinations of civil rights leader Martin Luther King Jr. and presidential hopeful Sen. Robert Kennedy (D-NY); the chaos of the Democratic National Convention in Chicago; and the emergence of a rare credible third-party presidential nominee in segregationist George Wallace, a Democrat who ran under the banner of the American Independent Party. And yet, despite all of the churn, very little changed in the House: Republicans netted just five seats, allowing Democrats to maintain their solid majority.

Redistricting may have contributed to the modest GOP gains in subtle ways. For instance, the House opted to prohibit statewide at-large

House districts in states that had more than one House member prior to the 1968 election, partly as a way to prevent states from using such districts as a way to dilute minority representation. Congress acted to promote "increased minority participation, political influence, and representation."[52] This impacted New Mexico, which prior to the House's statewide district prohibition had elected both of its House members at large. The adoption of districts combined with Nixon's strong showing in the state helped Republicans defeat both previously statewide Democratic House incumbents.[53]

The previously mentioned Texas redistricting prior to the 1966 elections gave further representation to the state's growing metropolitan areas, and the state modified the districts again in advance of 1968. One of the new districts created before the 1966 elections was TX-3, which covered West Dallas. Conservative representative Joe Pool (D) died, and wealthy businessman James Collins (R) won the district in an August 1968 special election and would hold this seat into the early 1980s. So here again is an instance of a Republican House victory that may have been owed at least in part to reapportionment boosting the representation of growing metropolitan areas in the South. Democratic presidential nominee Hubert Humphrey would narrowly win Texas in 1968, but Nixon ran about a dozen points ahead of his statewide share of the two-party vote in TX-3, meaning that the district voted considerably more Republican than both the nation and the state.

New York adopted new House districts under a court order in advance of 1968, starting a period of four straight House elections contested in the state under modified lines. The redistricting shuffled some districts, although the end result did not change the makeup of the state's 26–15 Democratic House delegation. However, that election did produce some notable new members of the House: Shirley Chisholm (D, NY-12), who in 1972 became the first Black woman to seek a major party presidential nomination, was elected to a new Brooklyn district drawn to be "all but certain to send a Negro to Congress."[54] Meanwhile, future mayor Ed Koch (D) won the wealthy and typically Republican "Silk Stocking" district in Manhattan, previously represented by liberal Republicans like John Lindsay, then mayor of New York City.

Next door in New Jersey, Republicans drew a new map to replace a temporary Democratic one, but despite preelection predictions suggesting that Republicans would make gains, they did not, although the map did preserve the two-seat gain Republicans had made in 1966.[55]

George Wallace's presence as a disruptive, southern-focused third-party candidate did not have any clear impact on the South's House delegation, even though Wallace comfortably carried 5 southern states (Alabama, Arkansas, Georgia, Louisiana, and Mississippi) and ran well ahead of his national share of the vote (13.5 percent) throughout the 11 states of the Old Confederacy. Republicans netted only two seats in the South in 1968—one was the aforementioned Texas seat that Collins technically won before the 1968 election, and the other was in North Carolina. That district (NC-5), created prior to the 1968 election in a Tar Heel State redistricting, was drawn as a competitive district.[56] It included both Winston-Salem and also some historically Republican northwestern turf in a state that otherwise was part of the Democratic "Solid South" (part of this district abutted eastern Tennessee, previously mentioned as a Republican southern outpost dating back to the Civil War). Wilmer "Vinegar Bend" Mizell (R), a former Major League Baseball pitcher, won the open seat in a close contest. Mizell was likely helped by Nixon's showing—Nixon carried the district with 48 percent of the vote, while Wallace and Hubert Humphrey (D) effectively split the remainder.

There were two other seats that flipped in the Greater South that year that effectively canceled each other out: a Democrat won an open Republican seat in West Virginia, and a Republican won an open Democratic seat in Virginia.

With Nixon in the White House, the generic midterm advantage typically enjoyed by the party not holding the White House shifted to the Democrats, although 1970 also was a year of only modest change in the House as the Democrats netted a dozen seats over the course of the cycle (some of these gains came in special elections in 1969, when long-serving Rep. David Obey of Wisconsin and a couple of other Democrats first won their seats). Among the Democratic victories were some oddities, like the Democrats winning both of South Dakota's districts, which were both Republican-held open seats. Democrats benefited from voters' displeasure with the Nixon administration's farm policies as well as from the eccentricities of the Republican candidate in SD-2, who wanted the government to create compulsory youth camps to teach "decency and respect for the law."[57] Observers cited farm policy as a reason for some of the other Democratic gains that year, such as in a northwestern Minnesota district (MN-7).[58] In fact, about half of the Democrats' total net gains came from the sparsely populated Interior West, of which northwestern Minnesota is not technically a part (but might as well be). Democrats netted the at-large seats in Alaska and Wyoming that year as well.

Redistricting had nothing to do with these gains, and the pace of district redrawing slowed in 1970 as states settled into *Wesberry*'s dictums. One of the few states to redistrict was New York, which was holding its final election before ceding to California the title of holding the nation's largest House delegation (California had passed New York as the most populous state in 1964[59] and has remained so ever since). The Supreme Court threw out the Empire State map in 1969, leading to gleeful Republican predictions that they would pick up a half-dozen seats or more thanks to a map created by the state's GOP-held government. "We can draw beautiful lines that can be as compact as a good cigar and still achieve a switch of six to eight seats for our side," an unnamed Republican redistricting expect predicted to the *New York Times*.[60] But despite skillful redistricting moves before the 1970 elections,[61] Republicans fell short of lofty predictions, netting only an extra two seats from New York: a number of popular Democrats in difficult districts nonetheless proved to be too well entrenched. One consequence of the new map was that it added some White liberal sections of Manhattan's Upper West Side to NY-18, a district centered on Harlem, a Black enclave represented by long-serving representative Adam Clayton Powell Jr. (D). Powell, who faced corruption allegations and had been excluded from taking his seat in the House (he eventually won a Supreme Court case to regain it), had been severely weakened. But he would have almost certainly won reelection had his district not been changed. As it was, Charlie Rangel (D) beat Powell by just 150 votes, and he won the new portion of the district by more than 1,500.[62] Rangel would serve in Congress for more than four decades. Another noteworthy new member of the New York House delegation elected in 1970 was Jack Kemp (R), a former Buffalo Bills quarterback who won an open seat in western New York. Kemp would become a prominent Republican thought leader on economic policy and was Bob Dole's running mate on the 1996 Republican presidential ticket.

1972: NIXON'S LONELY LANDSLIDE

House elected: 243–192 Democratic
Change from previous election: +12 Republican

In 1972, Nixon ran for reelection and benefited from a weak opponent, Sen. George McGovern (D-SD), an antiwar candidate who Nixon successfully pilloried as too far left. But despite Nixon's huge 60.7 percent to 37.5 percent national victory, Republicans only picked up a dozen House seats, a simple reversal of the Democrats' modest 1970 gains.

The GOP gains in 1972 might have been even smaller had it not been for the post-1970 reapportionment, which took effect in 1972. The reapportionment continued what would be a decades-long trend: generally faster growth in the Sun Belt pushed more House seats from the Northeast and Midwest to the South and West. There were exceptions, though. Alabama and Tennessee were among the losers in 1970, along with Iowa, North Dakota, Ohio, West Virginia, and Wisconsin. All lost one seat apiece. New York and Pennsylvania each lost two. Meanwhile, California gained five, Florida three, and Arizona, Colorado, and Texas one each. All told, the shuffle likely netted the Republicans an additional seat.

In the post-*Wesberry* era states now had to redistrict based on statewide population changes according to the decennial census, and nearly every state created new maps in advance of the 1972 election. As is clear from the modest net change overall, the redistricting did not lead to dramatic shifts in state US House delegations, although on balance Republicans seemed to catch more breaks than Democrats.

One favorable event for Republicans occurred in Illinois, where a federal court broke a legislative stalemate by adopting a map submitted by Republican state legislators, including future US representatives Henry Hyde and Edward Madigan.[63] The court's decision helped Republicans net an extra two seats in the Land of Lincoln. To the east in Indiana,

Republicans redrew IN-11 in Indianapolis to go after Rep. Andrew Jacobs Jr. (D). The remap worked, and minister William Hudnut III (R) narrowly defeated Jacobs, though he would win the seat back two years later.[64]

Other redistricting plans involved self-inflicted wounds. In Connecticut, Democrats ended up moving some Republican sections of CT-4 (a Republican-held seat) into CT-5, a Democratic seat they thought could take on additional Republican voters. Not only did Democrats fail to win CT-4, but adding more Republican voters to CT-5 allowed Republicans to win that district too.[65] Republicans also picked up a seat in Maryland, despite Democrats controlling the redistricting process, after the creation of MD-4, a district that connected the Baltimore and Washington, DC, suburbs but was dominated by Anne Arundel County (Annapolis). A Democratic remap in Tennessee did not perform as Democrats hoped,[66] allowing Republicans to take a five-to-three edge in the state's delegation. In Dallas' TX-5, conservative representative Earle Cabell (D) had a tough primary in 1970 and worked with allies in the state legislature to exclude some Black areas that had fueled the primary insurgency. Cabell's primary problems were solved, but removing some reliably Democratic voters probably hurt him in the general election, which he lost to a Republican. However, given that Cabell lost by a dozen points, he may have lost under the old lines too.[67]

Democrats did gerrymander effectively in other places. For example, in Massachusetts the Democratic state legislature eliminated some Republican territory from MA-12, the district covering Cape Cod. That prompted the conservative incumbent, Rep. Hastings Keith (R), who had already faced a spirited primary and general election challenge in 1970, to retire. Gerry Studds (D), Keith's 1970 opponent, ended up winning the seat.[68] Studds would serve for a quarter century, becoming the first openly gay member of Congress, a disclosure he made after the revelation of a sexual relationship with a 17-year-old male congressional page led to the House censuring him in 1983.[69] The same combination of Democratic-controlled redistricting and a tougher-than-expected challenge in the 1970 election prompted Rep. Page Belcher (R, OK-1) to retire in 1972, and James Jones (D), a former chief of staff to President Johnson, took his Tulsa-based seat. Republicans returned the favor in Colorado by targeting 12-term representative Wayne Aspinall (D, CO-4), who as chairman of the Interior Committee enraged environmentalists and attracted a primary challenger in 1970. State Republicans redrew his district, removing some of Aspinall's home base and adding some liberal-leaning areas. The shifts did the trick: Aspinall lost a primary, and then a Republican won the district in November.[70]

The South continued to show some signs of growing Republicanism. In Louisiana, David Treen (R) became the first Republican to represent that state in Congress in the 20th century, winning an open seat after two previous failed House bids and an unsuccessful gubernatorial run in 1971 (he would later win a single term as governor in 1979). Treen's victory, like other GOP House wins in the South, was fueled by strength in suburban areas (LA-3, the district he won, contained a significant portion of suburban New Orleans).[71]

In the wake of landmark civil rights legislation passed in the 1960s, Black voters emerged from their Jim Crow–enforced exclusion from the electorate in the South, and by 1972 their votes started to significantly affect results, both in electing Black members to the House and otherwise influencing elections, sometimes to the indirect benefit of Republicans.

In suburban Atlanta, court-ordered redistricting prompted one of the Republicans elected in the 1966 Georgia GOP breakthrough, Rep. Fletcher Thompson (R, GA-5), to unsuccessfully seek a Senate seat. The district, redrawn so as to be more amenable to electing a Black candidate, elected Andrew Young (D), a civil rights leader whom Thompson had defeated in 1970. Young would go on to serve as US ambassador to the United Nations and as mayor of Atlanta.

In Mississippi, two Republicans won election to the House: future senators Thad Cochran and Trent Lott. In Cochran's case, he won with just 48 percent of the vote, as an independent Black candidate took 8 percent of the vote. This was the first time in Mississippi that Black voters played a crucial role in the outcome of a congressional race.[72] And while her victory did not affect the overall House math in Texas, Barbara Jordan (D) won her first term to a Houston House seat that she maneuvered to have drawn for herself while she was serving in the Texas Senate.[73] Jordan and Young became the first Black candidates elected to the House from southern states in the 20th century.

Republicans also picked up two other southern seats with indirect assists from emerging Black electorates. In VA-4, long-serving conservative representative Watkins Abbitt (D) opted to retire after his home was drawn out of his district and as its composition of Black residents changed, potentially threatening him in a primary. He was replaced by a Republican.[74] In SC-6, another conservative House institution, Rep. John McMillan (D), lost a primary runoff in 1972 to a more liberal Democrat who won a large share of the Black vote.[75] Like in VA-4, a Republican replaced a conservative Democrat defeated in a primary, although the new Republican would lose to the liberal Democrat who beat McMillan in the rosier Democratic environment of 1974.

All in all, it is hard to argue with the assessment of political scientists Amihai Glazer, Bernard Grofman, and Marc Robbins in their analysis of the post-1970 redistricting round, at least in terms of the partisan makeup of Congress: "On balance congressional redistricting in the 1970s preserved the status quo; that is, neither party gained at the expense of the other."[76]

Republicans, meanwhile, made only a minor dent in the Democratic House majority, which had now gone uninterrupted since the Democrats retook the chamber in 1954 after a two-year hiatus. The GOP would fall farther behind in 1974, a classic midterm backlash year.

1974: THE WATERGATE WAVE

House elected: 291–144 Democratic
Change from previous election: +48 Democratic

Republicans got a preview of what awaited them in the 1974 midterm in a series of special House elections held in the first half of the year. Democrats won five previously Republican-held seats. That included the typically very Republican MI-5 based in Grand Rapids, which former House minority leader Gerald Ford (R) left behind when President Nixon made him vice president to replace Spiro Agnew, who resigned under the strain of legal questions. Among the special-election victors in 1974 was then state representative John Murtha (D) in PA-12, a western Pennsylvania district. Murtha would serve for more than 35 years in the US House.

Just like midterm elections generally, special US House elections break against the White House more often than they break toward it: according to a compilation of special-election results by *Bloomberg*'s Greg Giroux, 51 House seats flipped from one party to the other in the time frame covered by this book (starting in the 1964 election cycle). Of those 51 party changes, 38 saw the non–White House party flip a seat, while the president's party flipped only 13 seats.[77] Overall, special-election results can be indicative of what will happen in the subsequent general election. Political scientists David R. Smith and Thomas Brunell find that "when a party picks up more seats in a set of special elections than the other party gains, the more successful party can usually count on picking up seats in the next general election."[78]

One can see these dynamics when examining the special-election party flips in certain election cycles. For instance, Republicans flipped a total of six Democratic-held seats in special elections during the 1978 and 1980 cycles, and they made overall House gains in both elections. Democrats captured three strongly Republican-leaning seats in advance of their sweeping 2008 national victory. On the other hand, Democrats also picked up a couple of Republican-leaning seats in special elections held during 2004; yet Republicans held the White House and both chambers of Congress that year. So special elections are not always predictive of the future, but they can be.

In the 1974 election cycle, special elections—which function as a different kind of midterm election ("less regular and more idiosyncratic than others," as midterm expert Andrew Busch puts it)[79]—did end up being a harbinger of a big Democratic election to come later in 1974. Special elections are also notable, Busch wrote, not only because they garner a lot of attention from politicians and the media but also because the scarcity of special elections "elevates the importance of each one by focusing the eyes of the attentive public."[80]

Republicans were attentive to the special-election defeats that their party was suffering in the first half of 1974, and these electoral losses convinced many of them that Nixon needed to go[81] as the Watergate scandal engulfed his presidency. Nixon would resign in August, but his exit would not prevent big Republican losses that November when Democrats netted 48 House seats.

The maps used in the 1974 elections were generally the same as those used in 1972, although a few big states provided exceptions. New York's seemingly ever-changing maps again were modified (though only slightly and only within New York City). Much more importantly, California drew new maps after the state Supreme Court threw out a previous plan that essentially protected incumbents and divided the five new seats California added after the 1970 census (Democrats got three extra seats from reapportionment in California in the 1972 election, and Republicans got two). Under the new map, and with the political winds at their back, Democrats would net five new seats in California, giving them a 28–15 advantage in the largest House delegation. Texas, another megastate, also had to draw new districts because the US Supreme Court, in *White v. Weiser*, determined that the district populations "were not as mathematically equal as reasonably possible," thus reiterating the *Wesberry* standard.[82] In the short term, though, the new districts did not lead to much change: Democrats netted TX-13, a North Texas seat whose transformation had occurred in a previous redistricting.

Much of the rest of the Democratic gains seemed to be part of the usual midterm trend that was exacerbated in 1974 by Watergate. Democrats, for instance, netted five seats from Indiana, a typically Republican state then and now at the presidential level but at the time "a fairly good barometer of national opinion in state and congressional races."[83] The pro-Republican district maps in Illinois and New York collapsed under the burden of the Watergate wave as Democrats netted three seats from the Land of Lincoln and five from the Empire State. Minor redistricting completed in advance of the 1974 election did not contribute to the results in New York state: all of the Democratic gains came from outside the Five Boroughs, where districts were unchanged. Democrats picked up another five seats between 1972 and 1974 from Michigan, including Richard Vander Veen's (D) surprising victory in the MI-5 special. He held the seat in November. Another came from Rep. Don Riegle's decision in early 1973 to switch parties over the Vietnam War and other issues. Riegle ran for the Senate as a Democrat in 1976 and won the first of three terms.

Republicans lost ground all over the country, including in the South, losing eight net seats. Georgia reverted to a 10–0 Democratic delegation, and Republicans lost two seats apiece in North Carolina, Tennessee, and Virginia. Coming close to winning a House seat in 1974 was future president Bill Clinton (D), who challenged the aforementioned Rep. John Paul Hammerschmidt (R, AR-3) and lost by less than four points.

But there were Republican victories in the region too. In Florida's pre-1972 redistricting, the Democrats who ran the process created a new seat in central Florida designed to be won by state senator Bill Gunter (D). But he mounted an unsuccessful Senate bid immediately following his election to the House, and Richard Kelly (R) won the seat.[84] In Louisiana, Treen received some Republican reinforcement, although that new member did not technically win until 1975. Since 1967 the Baton Rouge–based LA-6 had been represented by Rep. John Rarick (D), "the most rabidly right wing member of the House" who "could be counted on to reprint in the *Congressional Record* just about any far right, anti-Semitic, or anti-black bilge that came across his desk."[85] Rarick's behavior was outrageous even for a conservative district, and he ended up losing the 1974 Democratic primary to Baton Rouge sportscaster Jeff LaCaze (D). He would face W. Henson Moore III (R), a conservative. A close result coupled with a voting machine problem prompted the Louisiana Supreme Court to order a new election, which Moore won in 1975. With Moore's victory, Republicans expanded their foothold in Louisiana, and this foothold endured and later expanded again—the state has elected at least two Republicans to the House in every election since 1974. And throughout the 2010s they held five of the state's six House seats.

❂ ❂ ❂

In comparing the Democrats' similarly sized House majorities of 1964 and 1974, one finds some contrasting trends in the regional distribution of the Democrats' power. The Democrats were strong throughout the period in both the Northeast and the West Coast, which would become the party's indisputable political strongholds by the 1990s. The sparsely populated Interior West was generally Republican in this period: a slim Democratic majority in 1964 was a clear aberration that was reversed to a comfortable GOP edge even in 1974. The Midwest, consistently a swing region, oscillated between the two parties in the House throughout this era, producing a majority Democratic delegation only in the big Democratic years of 1964 and 1974 and voting for more Republicans than Democrats in the intervening elections of 1966–72. And then there was the Greater South, which shifted from an overwhelming 105–19 Democratic majority in 1964 to a slightly less imposing 97–28. Democrats would largely rule the South for another two decades, but weaknesses were beginning to show. These regional shifts in the Democratic caucus are shown in figure 1.1.

Figure 1.1. Regional share of House seats won by Democrats, 1964–74

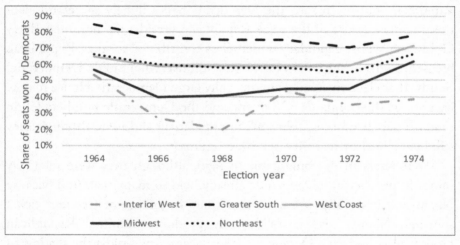

Source: Compiled by author

Did the Reapportionment Revolution have a major partisan impact? Likely not. Table 1.2 shows the House results in states that did and did not redistrict in 1964, 1966, and 1968, when states responded to the Supreme Court's one-person, one-vote mandate. As table 1.2 indicates, there's not a clear indication that one side or the other was disadvantaged by redistricting (or nonredistricting) in any of these three election cycles overall, although as noted throughout this chapter, individual state results varied.

Table 1.2. Net House change in states by districting status, 1964–68

	New districts?	No. of districts	Percentage of whole (435)	Net change	Total change	Share of total change
1964	Redistricted	61	14%	D +2	D +36	5%
	Not redistricted	374	86%	D +34		95%
1966	Redistricted	207	48%	R +23	R +47	49%
	Not redistricted	228	52%	R +24		51%
1968	Redistricted	203	47%	0	R +5	0%
	Not redistricted	232	53%	R +5		100%

Note: Some districts were redrawn more than once in this time frame; statewide, at-large districts are included in the "not redistricted" tally. *Source:* Compiled by author

Ultimately, the House elections in this period conformed largely to what one might have expected based on larger historical patterns in American politics. In 1964 the Democrats had a hugely successful election mainly because of the weak Republican presidential nominee, Barry Goldwater, whose candidacy nonetheless contributed to some Republican breakthroughs in the conservative (but still overwhelmingly Democratic) South. That election created an unusually large Democratic House majority even by the standards of that era, and the Democratic numbers fell in 1966 (in part because of Johnson's unpopularity) and 1968, although they still held a healthy majority in both elections.

Democrats made some gains in 1970, although they were relatively minor in part because Democrats already held so many seats and because Nixon was not really a drag at that time. In an age of frequent ticket splitting, Nixon's 1972 landslide only produced minimal Republican House gains, and then Democrats made large gains amidst the shadow of Watergate in 1974. The flood of new districts contributed to these shifts, but it's hard to say whether it made a huge impact on the size of either the Democratic or Republican House caucuses independent of the larger political trends of the era. District maps designed to help one side over the other, like New York's pro-Republican map in 1970, sometimes produced smaller gains than observers may have predicted. Others, like the Illinois map in 1972, helped Republicans that year but did not prevent Democrats from regaining lost ground two years later.

At the same time, reapportionment and redistricting did create new electoral opportunities. *Wesberry* provided more representation to growing suburban areas. This likely benefited Republicans in the South given that GOP strength was already percolating in the suburbs during this era. Yet the emergence of House Republicans in the South probably would have happened anyway. This is mainly because Republican gains in the South were not limited to suburban areas and were tied to other factors that had nothing to do with redistricting, including Goldwater's candidacy in 1964 and the slow but steady ideological realignment of the Democratic and Republican parties, which would continue for the rest of the 20th century and into the next.

Two

The Roots of the Republican Revolution

1976–94

In 1994, political scientists William F. Connelly Jr. and John J. Pitney Jr. released a book entitled *Congress' Permanent Minority? Republicans in the U.S. House.*[1] They were wise to include the question mark in their study: by year's end, the seemingly permanent minority had won the majority. One could hardly blame Connelly and Pitney—or anyone, really, including President Clinton—for wondering whether Republicans in the House might be a permanent minority. Not only had they not won the majority since the 1952 election, but they hadn't even reached 200 seats in the 435-seat body in any election since 1956.

So how did the Republicans finally win the House in 1994 after spending the previous four decades in the wilderness? Did their gains come all at once, or did they gradually build their path to the majority over time?

At the time it may have seemed that the Republican gains came almost all at once in the form of the GOP landslide in 1994. But what becomes clear through a long-range, district-by-district analysis is that the Republican House victories, for the most part, came gradually over the 1970s, 1980s, and early 1990s. During that time span the Republicans chipped away at the huge majorities the Democrats had won and maintained in the 1974 and 1976 elections. Republicans also held their ground in midterm elections during the presidencies of Ronald Reagan and George H. W. Bush, avoiding the kind of blowout seat losses that have often defined midterms for the presidential party. A combination of reapportionment, redistricting, and realignment helped build the Republican majority, as did a growing trend of partisan conflict and polarization. The Democrats' capture of the White House in 1992 was also a key ingredient in the Republicans' 1994 House victory, for reasons that a close reading of American electoral history makes clear.

REDISTRICTING, RACE, AND REALIGNMENT

The focus of this chapter is the Republican victory in 1994 and the roughly two decades of House elections leading up to this success starting in 1976. This section will assess some of the reasons why scholars believed the Democratic stranglehold on the House lasted as long as it did and what ultimately contributed to the Republicans finally taking control.

The Greater South looms large in this analysis. Indeed, a major factor in Democrats' continued House control into the 1990s was their ability to hold on to a healthy House majority with support from this region even as Republican presidential strength there grew.

In the 1976 presidential election, southerner Jimmy Carter's (D) sweep of the entire South outside of Virginia represented something of a last gasp for Democrats in southern presidential politics: Carter would be the last Democrat to win a majority of the electoral votes from a region that had long been heavily Democratic (albeit also very conservative). But the old Democratic "Solid South" had shown signs of erosion in the aftermath of World War II at the presidential level, and Barry Goldwater's 1964 presidential candidacy, in which he ran against federal civil rights legislation, allowed him to win several racially conservative southern states even as he was being defeated in a landslide nationally. Goldwater's small-government conservatism also stood in stark contrast to President Lyndon Johnson's liberalism on other issues, and conservative Republicans would eventually become a better fit for the conservative South than Democrats, liberal or otherwise. Goldwater's 1964 victory contributed to a small net increase in House Republicans from the South even as Republicans were losing about three dozen net seats nationally that year. Throughout the late 1960s and into the 1970s, Republican strength grew in the South, although by 1974 the GOP was up to only about a quarter of the seats in the South, as described in the previous chapter. That would grow to about a third in subsequent elections, but the Republicans found it difficult to get over that relatively small share throughout the 1980s. "Tracing the pace of Republican gains strongly suggests that partisan change was gradual," political scientist David Lublin argues, with key points of growth coming in 1964, 1980, and 1994. Democrats would recover after these elections, but they typically did not fully regain the ground they had lost, Lublin also observed.[2] This gradual pattern is apparent in figure 2.1, which shows the Republican seat share in the Greater South from 1964 to 2020. Notably, Lublin's earlier observation—Republicans making jumps at various points and then largely consolidating those gains—also seems present in the 2010s, as the GOP's share of districts in the Greater South spiked again in the party's 2010 wave (although it backslid a bit in the 2018 Democratic midterm victory).

Figure 2.1. Republican share of House seats in the Greater South, 1964–2020

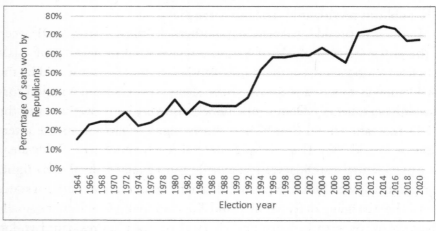

Source: Compiled by author

From 1953 to 1993, the Republicans held the presidency for 28 of a possible 40 years, and they won the presidency five out of six elections from 1968 to 1988. The South was very much a part of those victories. Yet there was a different story below the presidential ballot: "Since the late 1960s the persisting Democratic advantage at all levels of southern electoral politics below the presidential level has also successfully aborted the Republicans' efforts to realign the national party system,"[3] political scientist Nicol Rae writes. Even in Ronald Reagan's 1980 and 1984 presidential landslides, Democrats maintained control of the US House, aided by a large southern delegation. Southern Democrats were "consistently able to hold districts and states that ha[d] decisively rejected Democratic presidential candidates,"[4] Rae writes.

Part of the reason for lingering Democratic dominance in the South was the ability of Democrats to tailor their candidacies to local concerns: "A reputation for sensitivity to local interests [was] bread and butter to congressional Democrats," wrote House expert Gary Jacobson.[5] Another was the Republicans' failure to field strong candidates in the South (and elsewhere): "strong" candidates in this case being defined by Jacobson as ones who had held elective office prior to running for Congress. Throughout much of the 1950s through the 1980s, Democratic House challengers were more likely to have prior experience running for office.[6] Lublin agreed that "a lack of candidates impeded GOP efforts to expand their base of officeholders in the region for many years."[7]

Republicans also may have suffered, at least in the eyes of some of the party's internal critics in the 1970s and 1980s, from a lack of ambition in seeking the majority. Political scientist Frances Lee traced the rise of perpetual campaigning for Congress and the decline in bipartisanship to the 1980 election, when Republicans made major gains that opened their eyes to the possibility of winning the majority. They were incentivized to ditch bipartisanship and foster conflict that was "strategically engineered in the quest for political advantage as the two parties do battle for majority control" (Democrats, who had lost control of the Senate that year, took similar lessons from 1980).[8] In other words, the Republicans' recognition in 1980 that the Democratic majority in the House was not necessarily permanent may have prompted them to fight harder for the majority instead of acquiescing to working within the framework of the long-standing Democratic majorities.

The Democrats benefited from some structural advantages in the earlier part of this era, such as typically more influence over the congressional redistricting process. For instance, political scientist Alan Abramowitz found that in 1982 Democrats made more than half of their overall gains that year in the 17 states where they had complete control over the post-1980 census redistricting process.[9] In this era, Republicans were likelier to cry foul over partisan gerrymandering: President George H. W. Bush even proposed federal legislation in 1989 that would outlaw the practice.[10]

But Democrats found themselves on the wrong side of post-1990 redistricting in large part because of the creation of additional majority-minority congressional districts. Key legislative and judicial decisions in the 1980s prompted the US Department of Justice under Bush to push southern states, which had both significant minority populations and often required federal approval for redistricting, to create more districts with significant minority populations. The Justice Department had sway over these districts because of the Voting Rights Act's section 5, which stipulated that certain jurisdictions (including many southern states) receive DOJ preclearance for any voting changes they decide to make. That included new congressional districts.[11] Given that racial minorities, and Black voters in particular, vote much more often for Democrats as opposed to Republicans, the creation of such districts can "leave surrounding districts whiter and more conservative—and produce a net gain for the Republicans."[12] For Republicans, the push for majority-minority districts presented what legal expert and political scientist Maurice Cunningham argued was "the delicious irony of doing well while seeming to do good,"[13] meaning that Republicans could argue for a more diverse Congress and pursue a policy of majority-minority district maximization, knowing that it would benefit them electorally.

And it did. "There is evidence that Democrats lost about ten seats in 1994 due to racial redistricting," political scientist David Canon argued.[14] Cunningham pegged the scholarly consensus on Democratic losses in 1992 and 1994 because of racial redistricting at between 7 and 12 seats.[15]

Because the Republicans won 230 seats in the 1994 elections, they could have survived the loss of the net seats afforded them through racial redistricting. But their majority was smaller in subsequent Congresses, so it's possible that, without this racial redistricting, Democrats may have been able to win back the House sometime between 1994 and 2006, the dozen years when Republicans held power before the Democrats recaptured the chamber.

However, that also means that racial redistricting was not the decisive factor in the GOP's 1994 takeover, and that it was probably only a matter of time before the Republicans took a majority of the House seats in the South, which they finally did in 1994. Indeed, "One should emphasize that racial redistricting nevertheless remained a decidedly secondary problem for the Democrats compared to the more critical problem of white voters shifting to the GOP," Lublin argued.[16]

Other changes were afoot in this era. Divided government was the norm in the 1970s and 1980s, featuring largely Republican presidents, a Democratic House, and (mostly) a Democratic Senate: Republicans held that chamber from 1981 to 1987, while Democrats otherwise controlled it from 1955 to 1995. Therefore, Jacobson said that Americans simply became used to this governing arrangement, and liked it: Americans grew "increasingly content with divided control of the federal government"[17] and Democratic "control of Congress expresses, rather than thwarts, the popular will."[18]

Analysts in the late 1980s noticed the persistence of divided government and observed that there might be only one way for Republicans to take the House: a Democrat winning the White House. That's because changes in power in the House usually occur in midterm elections and involve the presidential party losing the majority: "The Republicans probably must lose a presidential election in order to position themselves to take a majority. . . . It is virtually impossible for a party to strengthen its position in the House at the same time that it occupies the White House,"[19] longtime congressional analyst Thomas Mann argued in the late 1980s. Since 1900, the House has flipped partisan control 11 times, and 9 of those turnovers occurred in midterm years, including the last five (1954, 1994, 2006, 2010, and 2018). "Without midterm elections," political scientist Andrew Busch argued, "divided government would be much less likely."[20] As noted in chapter 1, midterm losses for the party that controls the White House are a common feature of American politics; therefore, it's not unreasonable to conclude, as political scientist Robert Erikson did, that "losing the presidency is a stepping stone to midterm victory."[21] So something vital happened in 1992: Democrats, after a dozen years spent locked out of the White House, elected a president. Two years later, they lost the House.

House elected: 292–143 Democratic
Change from previous election: +1 Democratic

In the aftermath of the 200th anniversary of the signing of the Declaration of Independence, the United States hosted one of its most competitive presidential elections.

Carter, a former Georgia governor, won the national popular vote by about two percentage points over Gerald Ford (R), the unelected incumbent who took over after Richard Nixon (R) resigned in 1974. And the margins of Carter's victory were even narrower than that in Ohio and Wisconsin. Had these two states voted Republican, Ford would have had an Electoral College majority.

But despite the hotly competitive presidential race, the US Congress was dominated by Democrats. The party had held both the House and the Senate for more than two decades and enjoyed lopsided majorities in both chambers. In the House, Democrats netted a single seat, electing a 292–143 House majority.

That stability of the Democrats' House delegation was matched by a stability in the congressional district lines for the first time since the Supreme Court's reapportionment decisions upending congressional districting schemes that did not have equal population among districts. In every two-year election cycle since 1964, the first election since the reapportionment decisions, at least some states redrew their districting lines for one reason or another. But in 1976, the district lines were the same as they were in 1974—and would hold steady in 1978 and 1980 as well.

In the 1974 election, the Democrats won a clear majority of the House districts in four of the nation's five regions—the only exception was in the sparsely populated and usually conservative Interior West, where Republicans won 19 of 31 seats (less than 10 percent of the 435 total seats). Otherwise, Democrats held large majorities in the Northeast (75–38), the Greater South (97–28), and the West Coast (40–16), and they also were up 68–42 in the Midwest, a region where Republicans had generally held the majority over the previous decade. It is not a stretch to say that the Democrats dominated almost everywhere, not a surprising outcome when a party holds about two-thirds of all the seats.

The 1976 election shuffled the Democratic majority slightly, though its size remained constant. The biggest Democratic gain came in Pennsylvania, where the party netted three seats, mostly because they were able to win open seats after Republican incumbents retired. Democrats also netted two seats from Ohio, one because Don Pease (D) replaced liberal Republican Charles Mosher, who had retired from a northeast Ohio district (OH-13) that a normal Republican wouldn't have been able to hold. The other Democratic takeover in Ohio came in Cincinnati. Former representative Tom Luken (D) won one of the nationally watched 1974 Democratic special-election victories in OH-1 but then lost that November. He ran in a different Cincinnati-area seat and beat Rep. Don Clancy (R, OH-2).

Republicans netted individual seats in a handful of states. Some of their victories came against Democrats aided by the Watergate wave two years earlier, like Reps. Tim Lee Hall (D, IL-15) and Richard Vander Veen (D, MI-5). Vander Veen had won Ford's old Grand Rapids–based seat in a 1974 special-election shocker and then held it in the fall. But he could not hold on against Kent County Prosecutor Harold Sawyer (R) with Ford himself on ballot as the GOP presidential nominee in 1976. Another Republican winner in 1976 was Dan Quayle (R, IN-4), who would be elected to the Senate in 1980 and assume the vice presidency in 1988. Quayle beat a Democratic incumbent elected in 1970; the five newly elected Indiana Democrats who won amidst the Watergate wave there all held their seats two years later. That was a major story of the election: despite a few losses, the Democrats' 1974 Watergate class emerged from 1976 almost entirely intact.

Republicans did net two seats in the Greater South, winning open seats in Oklahoma City (OK-5) and Virginia's Northern Neck (VA-1). Republicans still effectively hold a version of the Virginia seat to this day, and they only lost control of the Oklahoma City seat in a 2018 upset, retaking it two years later. In a sign of slow Republican progress in the conservative (but still Democratic at this time) South, the GOP won 30 of the 125 seats in the region in 1976 as an evangelical Christian southern Democrat, Jimmy Carter, was sweeping the region outside of Virginia. Ten years earlier, Republicans had won an almost identical number—29 of 124—in the midst of 1966's national Republican midterm wave. Relative to national political trends, the Republicans were continuing to improve their standing in the Greater South.

The Democrats would never again reach large majorities like the ones they held in 1974 and 1976.

1978–80: REAGAN AND REPUBLICAN RENEWAL

House elected (1978): 277–158 Democratic
Change from previous election: +15 Republican
House elected (180): 243–192 Democratic
Change from previous election: +34 Republican

Given how huge the Democratic majority was and the usual midterm trend that almost always benefits the party that does not hold the White House, the Republicans' House gains in 1978—15 net seats gained from their 1976 showing—don't seem all that impressive. "House Republican candidates blew it," argued conservative *New York Times* columnist William Safire. This was partly because Democratic candidates had taken a conservative line on taxes.[22] Republicans focused their national campaign on an income tax cut proposed by Rep. Jack Kemp (R, NY-38) and Sen. William Roth (R-DE): "It was difficult to find a Republican nominee in any contested state or district who did not talk about Kemp-Roth," *Congressional Quarterly* noted in a recap of the election. However, Democrats argued that the tax cuts would increase inflation, proposing spending cuts instead, thus "co-opting normal Republican rhetoric."[23]

Midterm scholar Andrew Busch wrote that "observers noted at the time the degree to which the low partisan seat turnover masked a radical change in the agenda, a shift to the right that persisted through the 1980s and 1990s."[24] As Busch argued, the tone of 1978, defined by small government conservatism and tax revolt—most notably through California's June passage of Proposition 13, which imposed a two-thirds legislative majority requirement to raise taxes, among other limitations—offered a preview of conservative Ronald Reagan's (R) election as president two years later and a rightward shift in American politics.

A key figure in the political battles to come in the 1980s and 1990s, Newt Gingrich (R) first won election to the House as part of that year's new crop of Republicans. Gingrich was a college professor who had tried and failed to defeat a Democratic incumbent in a suburban Atlanta district in close contests in 1974 and 1976. Gingrich's persistence persuaded the Democrat, Rep. Jack Flynt (GA-6), to retire, giving Gingrich a clear path to the House. Gingrich was part of a five-seat net gain for Republicans in the Greater South, although the Republicans still won only 28 percent of the seats in the region. Republicans added a handful of seats from the Midwest, Northeast, and West Coast too. Some, like Gingrich, were emblematic of the party's combative, conservative, and southern-oriented future; others reflected the party's more moderate, northeastern past, like former state legislator Bill Green (R), who won a special election early in 1978 over former congresswoman and social activist Bella Abzug (D) in Manhattan after Rep. Ed Koch (D, NY-18) was elected New York City mayor in 1977. NY-18 covered the affluent Upper East Side area known as the "Silk Stocking" district. It generally preferred liberal Republicans, although it made an exception for Koch. Electing Green was a return to form even though Carter had won the district by 26 points in the 1976 presidential election. However, remember that nearly 30 percent of all districts had voted for different parties when choosing the president and House representative in 1976, so this sort of crossover representation was not unusual at the time. Green would serve until 1992, when he lost to a Democrat after the Silk Stocking district took on additional poor and middle-class neighborhoods in other New York City boroughs that were more reliably Democratic following redistricting; one Democrat quipped at the time that the district should be renamed the "Washed Denim" district.[25] Green remains the last Republican to represent Manhattan in the House.

Two other noteworthy first-time winners in 1978 were Geraldine Ferraro (D, NY-9), who would become the first woman on a major party presidential ticket when Democratic nominee Walter Mondale picked her in 1984, and Dick Cheney (R, WY-AL), who would go on to serve as House minority whip, secretary of defense under President George H.W. Bush, and vice president under President George W. Bush. Cheney, who had previously served as President Ford's chief of staff, flipped the Wyoming at-large seat to the Republicans following the retirement of Rep. Teno Roncalio (D).

Roncalio, who served nonconsecutive House stints from 1965 to 1967 and 1971 to 1978, remains the only Democrat to win a House election in the heavily Republican state in the post–World War II era.

The 1978 election would be the last time that Democrats won a House majority in a midterm held during a Democratic presidency. They have since failed to win a House majority in the four most recent midterms held under Democratic presidents, losing control of the House majority in 1994 and 2010 and failing to flip it from Republican control in 1998 and 2014.

Republicans gained even more seats in 1980, netting 34 across the country as Reagan defeated the unpopular, embattled Carter by about 10 points nationally and decisively in the Electoral College. Although the Democrats still had a 243–192 House majority, because of the large conservative contingent in the Democratic delegation—there were nearly 50 House Democrats who organized themselves as part of the "Conservative Democratic Forum" following the election[26]—Republicans had "effective control of the House, or something very close to it," wrote Michael Barone and Grant Ujifusa in the 1982 *Almanac of American Politics*.[27] The conservative lean of this particular Democratic caucus helped clear the way for Reagan's 1981 tax-cut package. "Like all politicians," the *Washington Post*'s Margot Hornblower and T. R. Reid observed in a 1981 feature on the newly constituted group of conservative Democrats, "their first impulse is survival and, in today's South, that often has little to do with the interests of the Democratic Party."[28]

The 1980 election results illustrated the inroads that Republicans were making in the South. Close to a third of the Republican gains came in the Greater South, representing another GOP leap in the region. Some of these gains would immediately fade away: for instance, Republicans won two of the four open seats in West Virginia, and Democrats quickly won them back in 1982. But others would endure for decades, like a GOP victory in SC-1, then (and now) a district based in stately Charleston that Democrats won in 2018 and then lost in 2020 and VA-10, a northern Virginia–based district that remained Republican until 2018.

Republicans drew even in the Midwest, notching a 55–55 tie in that competitive region's combined delegation (or a net gain of a half dozen seats). Several GOP gains there (and in other parts of the country) involved winning seats that had previously been Republican but that Democrats had won in 1974 and/or 1976. Those districts included IL-10 (a wealthy suburban seat covering some of Chicago's suburbs along Lake Michigan) and MN-6 (a district that extended from the state's southwest corner all the way to the Twin Cities suburbs). Both of these Republican pickups came after the Democratic incumbents, Reps. Abner Mikva (IL-10) and Rick Nolan (MN-6), decided not to run for reelection after winning these districts in the more favorable political climate of 1974.[29]

While those were open seats, Republicans largely beat Democratic incumbents to make their major gains in 1980, knocking off 27. Among the notable Democratic losers was Rep. Al Ullman (OR-2), a quarter-century member and chairman of the House Ways and Means Committee. He lost to Air Force veteran Denny Smith (R), who attacked Ullman for losing touch with the district and who likely benefited from Reagan's 19-point win in the eastern Oregon district, which covers most of Oregon's land mass and is Republican to this day. House majority whip John Brademas (D, IN-3), the number-three House Democrat, also lost in a district that Reagan won by 15 points. Brademas was defeated by John Hiler (R), a 27-year-old who had lost a state legislative primary two years before.[30] Rep. Gunn McKay (D, UT-1) ran 26 points ahead of Reagan in his district but still lost by four points to Utah state house speaker James Hansen (R). Another prominent Democrat who lost was veteran liberal representative James C. Corman (D, CA-21), the chairman of the Democratic Congressional Campaign Committee. He lost to Bobbi Fiedler (R), who rose to prominence as an opponent of busing to desegregate schools.[31]

Also contributing to Republican gains in 1980 was Abscam, an FBI sting operation that involved fake Arab sheikhs offering bribes to lawmakers.[32] The sting ensnared six members of the House, five of whom were Democrats. Republicans defeated three of them in November 1980: Reps. Frank Thompson (NJ-4), John Murphy (NY-17), and John Jenrette (SC-6). So Republicans effectively netted three seats from Abscam. One of those members elected against an Abscam-damaged member, Chris Smith (R, NJ-4), was reelected in 2020 to his 21st term.

While Republicans did not win the House in 1980, the narrowing of the Democratic edge (and the Republican victory in the Senate) "dramatically raised House Republican hopes," wrote Frances Lee in her analysis of party competition in Congress. And even before that victory, some younger members like Gingrich had been agitating for the party to take a more aggressive stance against the Democrats. "An increasing number of Republicans embraced this critique over time, and the confrontationalist faction had prevailed by 1989," Lee added.[33] That year, 1989, was marked by Gingrich's victory in the Republican caucus race to become minority whip, a position he narrowly won over Ed Madigan of Illinois. As political scientist Douglas Harris argued in an analysis of the vote, individual members took into account Gingrich's confrontational style versus Madigan's desire for accommodation and, by a slim 87–85 vote, backed Gingrich—and thus confrontation.[34]

However, from the perspective of 1980, it would still be some time before confrontational Republicans like Gingrich would take command of the Republican caucus. In the aftermath of Reagan's victory, House Republicans picked the accommodating Rep. Bob Michel (R, IL-18) as minority leader, a selection that to Gingrich "signaled that his party remained resigned to the life of a permanent minority."[35] Throughout the 1980s, the Republicans found themselves stymied in their efforts to win a majority.

1982: The Democratic Comeback

House elected: 269–166 Democratic
Change from previous election: +26 Democratic

After cutting the Democratic margin substantially in the House in 1980, some Republicans made their feelings clear about taking the majority in 1982. In June 1981, Republican National Committee chairman Richard Richards "flatly promised a House takeover."[36] Yet even a basic understanding of American political history would have suggested this was highly unlikely: even in the few instances in modern American political history when the president's party has gained seats in a midterm, the size of those gains has been in the single digits, whereas the Republicans needed to pick up 26 seats to win the House. What actually happened was more predictable based on history. The Democrats picked up 26 seats instead, as Reagan and the Republicans dealt with a deep recession, the usual White House midterm drag, and new House maps that largely helped Democrats.

The 1980 census congressional reapportionment continued to shift House seats from the Northeast and Midwest to the faster-growing West and South. Florida was the biggest gainer, adding four seats, followed by Texas adding three additional seats. New York was the biggest loser, with its delegation dropping five seats, while other Frost Belt states—Illinois, Ohio, and Pennsylvania—lost two apiece. All in all, the Northeast lost nine House seats and the Midwest lost seven, while the Greater South gained eight and the West Coast and Interior West gained four apiece. Ultimately, a seat-by-seat comparison of seats gained and lost across the affected states netted the Democrats five seats. And then there was redistricting, a state-by-state process from which Democrats benefited more than Republicans. Journalist Michael Barone argued that redistricting "probably" netted the Democrats 15 seats in 1982 in states where they held sway,[37] and political scientist Alan Abramowitz concurred.[38]

A "grotesquely-shaped" and highly consequential partisan gerrymander came in California, where Rep. Philip Burton's (D, CA-5) new map helped turn a 22–21 Democratic edge in the California delegation into a 28–17 advantage: the map featured two new Democratic districts, and many others had been altered to Democrats' benefit.[39] A Democratic gerrymander in Texas also allowed the Democrats to sweep the state's three new seats. Meanwhile, GOP-controlled redistricting was both less common and less effective. Despite creating what *Congressional Quarterly* referred to in a headline as a "classic gerrymander,"[40] Indiana Republicans took a 6–5 Democratic delegation and produced a map that produced a 5–5 split, meaning that Democrats lost just a single seat. Democrats held the line in Indiana in part because Bloomington mayor Frank McCloskey (D) unseated Rep. Joel Deckard (R, IN-8) in that frequently competitive district (Deckard hurt his reelection bid with a drunken driving crash prior to the election).[41] The "Bloody Eighth" threw out seven different incumbents in roughly a half century before settling down as a more reliably Republican district in the 2010s.[42] The district would figure prominently in the 1984 House elections, and it wouldn't be until 1994 that Indiana Republicans would win a majority of the state's seats. Republicans also controlled redistricting in Pennsylvania, but it was the GOP who ended up losing the two seats necessitated by reapportionment. One of the seats the Democrats effectively held was a western Pennsylvania seat held by Rep. Eugene Atkinson (PA-4), who switched from Democratic to Republican in 1981 only to lose to a Democrat in a 1982 landslide. One other party switcher, conservative representative Bob Stump (R, AZ-3), easily kept his seat. A couple of additional party switchers would show up in the next cycle: conservative representative Andy Ireland (R, FL-10) switched parties and easily won reelection in 1984, and Rep. Phil Gramm (R, TX-6) also switched and then won a Senate seat in 1984 (and was replaced by a Republican, Joe Barton, who went on to serve for nearly a quarter century before retiring in advance of the 2018 election).

Democrats benefited from the courts in Illinois, which had drawn a map that favored Republicans in the 1970s but picked a Democratic plan for the 1980s,[43] and also in Minnesota, where Democrats turned a 5–3 Republican edge into a 5–3 Democratic advantage. A bipartisan plan in New York ended up with the Democrats losing just two seats to the Republicans' three as the state reckoned with reapportionment losses. One of the few bright spots for Republicans across the nation came in Ohio, where a bipartisan redistricting plan did nothing to help Rep. Bob Shamansky (D, OH-12), who surprisingly defeated a longtime Republican incumbent in the Columbus-area district in 1980. But neither Democrats nor Republicans in state government got along with Shamansky, and the new redistricting plan helped then state senator John Kasich (R) become the only Republican challenger to beat a Democratic incumbent in 1982.[44] Kasich would go on to become an influential House member, Ohio's governor from 2011 to 2019, and an unsuccessful presidential candidate in 2016 who crossed party lines to back Democrat Joe Biden in the 2020 presidential race.

Redistricting did not have much effect on some of the Democratic gains, which in some cases represented an ebbing of the Reagan tide that flipped some lost 1980 districts back to Democrats in 1982. So some Democratic losers in 1980, like Bob Carr (MI-6) and Peter Kostmayer (PA-8), regained their seats in the better conditions of 1982.

Combining their gains from reapportionment and redistricting suggests that the map changes, at the very least, accounted for a significant portion of Democrats' 1982 gains. There was also the poor state of the economy: the Federal Reserve's official history classified the 1981–82 downturn as the worst recession the nation suffered between the Great Depression and the more recent 2007–9 recession.[45] Given redistricting and recession, the Democratic gains were less than impressive. Midterm expert Andrew Busch noted that during two previous recession-aided midterms (1958 and 1974), the losses of the presidential party were almost double those of 1982 (48 seats in each election). One factor, suggested by House experts Gary Jacobson and Jamie L. Carson, may be that Democratic challengers were not as well funded as Republican challengers in 1982.[46] This squares with a larger observation from Jacobson and Carson, which is that campaign spending is more important for challengers than incumbents because the money spent in support of challengers "buys the attention and recognition that incumbents already enjoy at the outset of the campaign."[47]

Busch argued that two major theories began to circulate around the 1982 results: one was that the results were not a broad repudiation of President Reagan but rather more of a course correction; the second was that despite somewhat disappointing gains, the character of the House had changed to the extent that "the Democratic leadership had regained effective control of the House" from the alliance of Republicans and conservative Democrats.[48]

1984–90: YEARS OF STASIS

House elected (1984): 253–182 Democratic
Change from previous election: +16 Republican
House elected (1986): 258–177 Democratic
Change from previous election: +5 Democratic
House elected (1988): 260–175 Democratic
Change from previous election: +2 Democratic
House elected (1990): 268–167 Democratic
Change from previous election: +8 Democratic

The four elections following 1982 were years of relative tranquility in the partisan makeup of the House. The Republicans regained some of their losses in 1984, netting 16 seats in the midst of Reagan's landslide reelection.

The following three elections saw Democrats net five seats in 1986, two in 1988, and eight in 1990. So over the course of four elections, the net change in the House was just a one-seat Republican gain.

Contributing to the low levels of net partisan change were largely stable maps throughout the decade after 1982, when every state with more than one district—with the exception of Maine and Montana—redistricted. (The M&M laggards, two sparsely populated states with just two districts apiece, would redistrict to little fanfare in 1984.) California Democrats also tweaked their gerrymander after voters threw out the old "Burtonmander," although the changes were minor (outgoing Democratic governor Jerry Brown signed the new map into law just before departing office in early 1983). The only change in California was a single GOP gain in 1984: Bob Dornan (R), a former House member and talk show host who had unsuccessfully run for the Senate in 1982, moved to an Orange County district (instead of running for reelection in a Los Angeles County seat) and beat Rep. Jerry Patterson (D, CA-38). "B-1 Bob" Dornan, nicknamed as such for his outspoken advocacy of the B-1 bomber project, won 53 percent of the vote in a district the Californian Reagan carried with 69 percent. Burton died in 1983 and was replaced by his wife, Sala, in a special election for his San Francisco seat. She died four years later and was replaced by future Democratic Speaker of the House Nancy Pelosi in another special election.

More helpful to Republicans than the slightly adjusted Golden State map was a new map in Texas forced by a court ruling. Republicans would gain five seats in Texas in 1984, aided by Reagan's sweep and the new lines but also by the fact that Republicans were beginning to have more success winning support for their candidates at the congressional level, not just statewide.[49] After 1984, the Texas delegation was 17–10 in favor of Democrats. Republicans had reached double digits there for the first time in history. They would fall back in a few places over the rest of the decade, but they had already come a long way since 1976—when they won just 2 of the 24 seats in the Lone Star State—and even further from 1964, when they were shut out of the state's House delegation entirely. Texas would eventually become one of the crucial power centers of the GOP House delegation, and two of the Texans first elected in 1984—Dick Armey (R,

TX-26) and Tom DeLay (R, TX-22)—would both later serve as House majority leader. A court-ordered map in New Jersey that replaced a previous Democratic gerrymander directly led to the defeat of Rep. Joseph Minish (D, NJ-11), a long-serving but unaccomplished member.[50]

Additionally, Republicans seemed to benefit from the delayed effects of previous redistricting. In other words, they gained some seats in 1984 that they arguably could have (or should have) won in 1982. For instance, a Republican-drawn map in Arizona that failed to deliver a new seat to the party in 1982 performed better in 1984, giving the Republicans a delayed pickup two years earlier. A lagging redistricting effect probably helped the Republicans pick up a seat in Maryland, and in North Carolina, a court-modified House map made to comply with the federal Voting Rights Act was supposed to help the Republicans in 1982,[51] but Democrats ended up netting two seats instead. Congress had modified the VRA in 1982 in such a way that it would be, according to *New York Times* reporter Robert Pear, "read as requiring states to create districts with black and Hispanic majorities wherever possible,"[52] although a big federal push for majority-minority districts would not come until the 1990 redistricting cycle. Republicans returned fire in 1984 in the Tar Heel State, picking up three seats as six races overall were decided by two points or less (Republicans won four of the six). So redistricting, conducted both before and after 1982, helped the Republicans gain some ground in 1984. But these gains were tenuous.

In Indiana's "Bloody Eighth," a razor-thin race between first-term representative Frank McCloskey (D) and state representative Richard McIntyre (R) led to a divisive battle in the House itself over how to handle the race. The Indiana secretary of state, a Republican, certified McIntyre as the victor by 34 votes, but Democrats cried foul over a partial recount that seemed to benefit McIntyre. On a party-line vote, House Democrats decided to keep the seat vacant, and their own investigation concluded that McCloskey had won by four votes. Republicans howled in protest, but that did not prevent the Democratic majority in the House from voting to seat McCloskey, although a handful of Democrats voted against seating him. The bare-knuckle battle provided fuel to the confrontationalist faction of the GOP, led by Gingrich, who wanted the GOP House minority to take a harder line against a Democratic House leadership that they believed had wronged them in the battle over the IN-8 results.[53]

The House now stood at 253–182, and the Republicans didn't have realistic prospects for winning the majority in 1986 given that Reagan was still in the White House. This meant that the Democrats continued to benefit from the usual out-party midterm pattern.

The Democrats did end up winning the Senate in 1986, capturing the majority after the Republicans had won it in 1980, but there wasn't much of an overall wave. The 1981–82 recession had long passed, and Reagan was popular; the Iran-Contra scandal that would tarnish the final two years of his presidency broke immediately after the midterm and had no effect on that election. The Democrats picked up a modest five seats in the House, few of which were notable. A district in Mississippi that had been drawn to elect a Black candidate to satisfy the VRA failed to do so in both 1982 and 1984. But in 1986, attorney Mike Espy, a Black Democrat, won the seat. Additionally, another VRA district in Atlanta elected civil rights activist John Lewis (D, GA-5) in 1986 after a White Democrat, Wyche Fowler, had previously held the seat (Fowler won a Senate race that year). Elsewhere in the South, Democrats won back two of three seats they had lost in North Carolina. So the map designed to favor the GOP didn't deliver in 1986. In Oklahoma, James Inhofe (R), a future US senator, won the Tulsa-based OK-1 after Rep. James Jones (D) ran for Senate (Jones had won a close reelection in 1984 as Reagan was carrying the district by 41 points). Republicans had held a version of OK-1 prior to Jones's initial victory there in 1972, and they have held OK-1, under changing lines, ever since.

Two years later, as George H. W. Bush's election meant a third straight term for Republicans in the White House, there was also little change in the US House, as Democrats netted two seats.

As part of that year's small seat exchange, Republicans netted two seats in Florida as they captured an open seat and also saw a political newcomer, Craig James (R), topple Rep. Bill Chappell (D, FL-4), a 20-year incumbent saddled with ethics problems. Early in Bush's presidency, state senator Ileana Ros-Lehtinen (R) would win a special election following the death of longtime representative Claude Pepper (D, FL-18) for a Miami-based seat with a large Cuban population. Not only would

Ros-Lehtinen hold a version of the seat for nearly three decades—she retired ahead of the 2018 election when her seat flipped to the Democrats and then back to the Republicans in 2020—but her victory, plus the two seats the GOP netted in 1988, gave Republicans a majority of Florida's House seats. Republicans have held a majority of Florida's House seats ever since, as the growing state has increased the size of its delegation.

Importantly for House Republicans, even as they continued to labor in the minority, they finished the eight years of Reagan's presidency having suffered little net loss. Starting from the 1980 election—one in which the Republicans, again, netted 34 seats—they only lost a total of 17 House seats from Reagan's inauguration through Bush's inauguration. Those are the fewest seats lost by any presidential party over the course of all the post–World War II two-term presidencies and significantly fewer than the average (40 seats) losses inflicted on the eight postwar administrations (this analysis counts as a single administration the John F. Kennedy/Lyndon B. Johnson presidencies from 1961 to 1969 and the Richard Nixon/Gerald Ford presidencies from 1969 to 1977).[54] In other words, the Republicans more than held their own in the House during the Reagan presidency given the usual toll holding the White House inflicts on down-ballot fortunes. The relative stasis in the House continued in 1990, when Democrats made another relatively minor gain despite not holding the presidency (eight seats, after their small five-seat gain in 1986).

Indiana Republicans, who had tried to draw themselves a favorable map in advance of the 1982 election, saw Democrats net two seats in the Hoosier State, so the party, on what seemed like the wrong end of a gerrymander, finished the decade holding 8 of Indiana's 10 seats. Republican growth in the South, meanwhile, continued to be sluggish: Democrats still held the majority of the seats in 12 of the 14 states of the Greater South (the Old Confederacy plus Kentucky, Oklahoma, and West Virginia). The exceptions were the aforementioned Florida delegation (narrowly controlled by Republicans) and Louisiana (a four-to-four split).

One narrow Republican survivor in 1990 was Gingrich, who defeated a Democratic challenger by less than a percentage point. Gingrich's national profile was continuing to grow—he had played a major role in publicizing a scandal that prompted Speaker of the House Jim Wright (D, TX-12) to resign in 1989—but according to historian Julian Zelizer, "the exuberance that Washington seemed to feel toward Gingrich did not translate to his district, where some wondered why he spent so much time on his national aspirations as opposed to the bread-and-butter needs of his constitu-ents."[55] As it was, Gingrich survived—but he was the only Republican in the Georgia House delegation. That would change two years later.

1992: Racial Redistricting and Turnover Boost Republicans

House elected: 259–176 Democratic
Change from previous election: +9 Republican

The ongoing shift in population growth from north and east to south and west was confirmed once again in the 1990 census, with New York losing another three seats while big northern industrial states Illinois, Michigan, Ohio, and Pennsylvania lost two apiece. Gaining representation was California, which added seven seats, as well as Florida (four) and Texas (three). The population changes, along with an improved redistricting picture nationally—the Republicans were still at a national disadvantage against the Democrats, but they were in better shape than they had been in post-1980 redistricting thanks in part to some success in 1990s guber-natorial races[56]—meant that in 1992 Democrats seemed destined to lose one to two dozen seats.[57]

But the Democrats came out roughly even in the exchange of seats be-tween the states losing seats and those gaining, in part because the Dem-ocrats still controlled the levers of redistricting power in some key states like Texas, where the *Almanac of American Politics* awarded Democrats the decade's "Phil Burton Award" for their pro-Democratic gerrymander.[58] Democrats ended up winning all three of the new Texas seats and only losing one of their other seats, giving them 21 of 30 seats in a state that was clearly trending Republican; it had voted by double-digit margins for Reagan in 1980 and 1984 and home state candidate Bush in 1988 and would resist Bill Clinton (D) in both 1992 and 1996 despite the former Arkansas governor winning two clear victories nationally those years.

Clinton's win over President Bush in 1992, which was complicated by businessman Ross Perot's strong showing as an independent (he won al-most 19 percent of the national popular vote, although he won no electoral votes), may have also helped Democrats outperform House expectations in 1992. For instance, the writers of the *Almanac* argued that Bush's "collapse" on the West Coast "helped Democrats win about nine districts there that Republicans expected to take."[59] All told, Republicans netted nine seats, which was not bad when one considers that they would go on to lose the White House for the first time in a dozen years.

The big story in redistricting in 1992 was the Bush administration's push to create majority-minority districts based on the Voting Rights Act. There was a political impetus here: Republicans had come to believe that creating new majority-minority districts would create heavily Democratic districts, leaving surrounding districts more Republican.[60] The result was the creation of 15 new majority Black districts and 10 new Hispanic majority districts after the 1990 round of redistricting.[61] There were political costs to Democrats in the new maps, some of which would become apparent in the 1992 elections.

For instance, in Florida a new majority-Black district connecting Jacksonville to Orlando allowed state representative Corrine Brown (D) to win election to the House. But the removal of Black voters from Jacksonville-area representative Charles Bennett's (D, FL-4) district made the long-serving member's reelection bid trickier, and he announced his retirement, citing his wife's health. Bennett's retirement opened a seat that Jacksonville city councilwoman Tillie Fowler (R) won.[62] In Alabama, Rep. Ben Erdreich's (D, AL-6) district went from 37 percent Black to 9 percent Black as a new majority-Black district was created elsewhere in the state. The district thus became more Republican, and Erdreich lost to Spencer Bachus (R).[63] In Georgia, Democrats constrained by the VRA-district push and population growth in the heavily Republican Atlanta suburbs meant there was no way to draw a map that would only elect one Republican. But Democrats tried to draw the map in such a way that Gingrich would lose; not only did he run in a different district and win, but Republicans ended up winning 4 of the state's 11 seats.[64]

Two other factors are worth noting from 1992. Firstly, that year featured a lot of turnover, as just 368 of the 435 districts featured an incumbent running for reelection, the lowest total of the post–World War II era.[65] There were many reasons for the high number of open seats: 1992 was a redistricting year, which often creates more turnover and sometimes leads to members running against members in the same district. The

House also was rocked by the House banking scandal, in which hundreds of members wrote overdrafts on House checking accounts. The bank had covered the checks and thus issued "in effect, interest-free loans to members with negative balances."[66] According to political scientists Michael Dimock and Gary Jacobson, the scandal depressed the performance of House incumbents by about five percentage points and likely contributed to at least some incumbent losses.[67] As a result of all the turnover, 110 new members were elected to the House in 1992.[68]

The other factor worth noting is that more than half of the nation's districts were drawn either in a bipartisan way by state governments under divided party control or in a nonpartisan way, like a commission in Washington State that drew a highly competitive map where Democrats captured eight of the state's nine seats in 1992.[69] So while Republicans did not initially make huge strides as the decade's race for the House began, they were in a strong position to make gains if the political environment cooperated as Clinton's presidency began. As it turned out, the environment *did* cooperate.

1994: The Fall of the Democrats

House elected: 230–205 Republican
Change from previous election: +54 Republican

A confluence of factors conspired to make the Democratic House majority highly vulnerable in 1994. For starters, the Democrats now held the White House again for just the second time since the end of Lyndon Johnson's presidency. Over the course of a quarter century, they had only dealt with a single midterm election while controlling the White House: that midterm was in 1978, when they avoided major losses even as the election augured poorly for liberalism's near future. The Republicans, meanwhile, had to defend their House caucus in five such midterms over the same period. As previously noted, in the late 1980s House experts Gary Jacobson and Thomas Mann posited that the Democratic House majority might be vulnerable the next time Democrats held the White House during a midterm election.

Republicans, now holding no levers of power in Washington, decided that they would not work with Democrats. Gingrich, who had become minority whip in the close 1989 caucus election, and other Republican leaders decided that cooperating with the Democratic House majority was not going to help them win their own majority.[70] Republicans, therefore, provided no votes for a budget bill that included tax increases in Clinton's first year. Democrats narrowly passed the budget through the House, with first-term representative Marjorie Margolies-Mezvinsky (D, PA-13) providing a decisive vote. As Margolies-Mezvinsky cast her vote, Republicans chanted "Bye-bye Marjorie" on the House floor (and she would in fact lose in 1994). A contributor to Bush's 1992 loss arguably was his broken pledge not to raise taxes, and his reversal "had torn [Bush's] party apart" in 1990, as political analyst Steve Kornacki argues in his history of 1990s partisan conflict. This time, Republicans held their ground against a tax bill and anticipated political gains from it.[71]

Clinton and the Democrats also tried and failed to substantially increase health insurance coverage. "The health-care fiasco only added fuel to the Republican contention that the institution had been corrupted by continuous Democratic rule for the past forty years," writes official House historian Robert Remini, who also noted the effects of the House banking affair and other scandals, including one that ensnared powerful Democratic House Ways and Means Committee chairman Dan Rostenkowski (D, IL-5).[72] Rostenkowski, indicted on embezzlement and fraud charges, lost his committee chairmanship and, later, his 1994 reelection bid in his otherwise very Democratic-leaning district. Meanwhile, Clinton's approval rating sank to the low to mid 40s during the months leading up to the election.[73]

The party polarization and straight-ticket voting that would come to be so prevalent in the 21st century began to show itself, subtly, in 1992. One hundred House districts still voted for different parties for president and House. But that was actually the lowest number of crossover House districts since 1952, and the number would dwindle over time. In the aftermath of 1992, the *Almanac of American Politics* picked up on an emerging trend of the nationalization of politics and argued that House Democratic candidates in 1992 had campaigned on many of the same issues that Clinton had that year, instead of focusing on "the sort of local and micro-issues which House members of both parties have used to help them weather difficult years for their parties in marginal districts."[74] This trend on the Democratic side in 1992 dovetailed with what Kornacki describes as an overarching Gingrich strategy, which was "finding a way to nationalize congressional elections" against Democrats, who had benefited from the power of incumbency and a separation between perceptions of the national party and perceptions of individual Democratic House members.[75]

Meanwhile, among southern White voters, Republican self-identification finally surpassed Democratic self-identification, just as racial redistricting with the goal of creating majority-minority districts was reshaping the southern congressional map, with heavily Democratic Black voters being packed together in districts designed to elect Black Democrats. That left southern White Democrats in the position of having to defend Whiter and more Republican districts than what they were used to, just as White southerners were becoming less likely to identify as Democrats.

For Democrats, all of this was a toxic brew. And the GOP hammer fell hard.

Republicans smashed Democrats in several regions of the country, netting 54 seats. Some of their biggest net gains came in southern states where Democrats had held on in 1992 despite the constraints of the VRA, but those maps could not withstand the Republican wave in 1994. Republicans netted three seats in Georgia and four in North Carolina, winning control of those states' House delegations for the first time in post-Reconstruction history. Republicans also netted two seats apiece in Kentucky, Tennessee, and Texas, although the VRA wasn't really a factor in those losses. A Democratic gerrymander in Oklahoma retained the state's four-to-two Democratic House delegation in 1992, but in 1994 it fell apart as the GOP netted three seats (all of which were open). All told, the Republicans netted 21 seats in the Greater South, taking a slim majority (73–67) of the seats in the region for the first time in modern history.

But the gains were not limited to the South. Surveying the wreckage of the Democrats' lost majority, R. W. Apple Jr. of the *New York Times* observed that the Republican gains "were centered mainly on suburban and small-town areas that are arguably naturally Republican, and had been held by Democrats mainly through superior skills."[76] Therein lay the logic of the Gingrich nationalization strategy and also the precarious position in which Democrats found themselves in a time of high House turnover. Republicans won 22 previously Democratic open seats, and they beat another 11 first-term Democratic incumbents, which meant that a clear majority of their gains came in seats where the power of incumbency was either absent or not deeply rooted.

The competitive Washington State map, which had elected an eight-to-one Democratic delegation in 1992, gave the Republicans a net gain of five seats in 1994. One of the losers, in a right-of-center eastern Washington district, was Speaker of the House Tom Foley (D, WA-5), the first sitting speaker to lose in the post–Civil War era. Foley had taken over as speaker in 1989 following Jim Wright's resignation. Republicans also netted three seats in California and two in Arizona, making some of the gains in 1994 many had expected them to make in 1992. They netted 12 in the competitive Midwest, retaking the majority in that region's combined delegation. In Indiana, Republicans finally retook the state's delegation, netting three seats and winning a six-to-four advantage on a map that hadn't changed much since their gerrymander way back in 1982. The Republicans' other big midwestern gains came in Ohio, where they netted four seats. The one region where Republicans hardly picked up any ground was the Northeast, where they netted only three seats. The shifts in Democratic control over the course of the 1976–94 period are shown in figure 2.2. Note the regional confluence outside of the more Republican Interior West. Although the southern results represented a breakthrough for Republicans, the GOP nonetheless built its majority in a regionally broad-based way, with sharp downticks for Democrats in four of the five regions.

Figure 2.2. Regional share of House seats won by Democrats, 1976–94

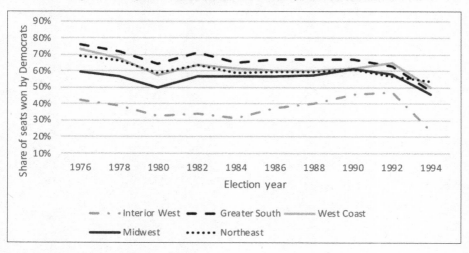

Source: Compiled by author

Still, what may not have been completely clear at the time (but is certainly clear now) is that the Republicans had hardly maximized their gains in the South. The Democratic gerrymander was still in place in Texas, giving them a 19–11 majority there even after the GOP picked up two seats. In conservative states like Alabama, Louisiana, and Mississippi, Democrats retained House delegation majorities. But these majorities wouldn't last.

* * *

The late 1970s and 1980s were largely frustrating times for Republicans in their efforts to win the House. Holding the White House proved to be a burden for Republicans, preventing them from making the House gains that midterm elections often produce for the party that doesn't hold the presidency. That said, Democrats found themselves unable to maintain their huge majorities of 1974 and 1976, when they elected about two-thirds of the entire House each time. And Democrats failed to build majorities large enough to put the House out of reach for Republicans when they had their own midterm opportunities, particularly in 1986 and 1990. The confluence of numerous open and vulnerable seats, racial redistricting and realignment in the South, and an unpopular presidential administration trying to defend its majority in a midterm helped Republicans break the Democratic hammerlock on the House in 1994.

THREE

The House from 1996 to 2020

A Persistent but not Unassailable Republican Edge

The election of 1994 represents a dividing line between two eras in the House. In the 63 years prior to that election, the Democrats would hold the majority for 59 years. In the 28 years following 1994—through the upcoming 2022 election—Republicans would hold the majority for 20 years. Figure 3.1 shows the partisan breakdown in the House from 1964 to 2020. Note the shift in 1994 from a long era of Democratic control to a time when Republicans have been likelier to hold the majority. But as of this writing, the Democrats controlled the House, albeit with just a narrow 222–213 majority elected in 2020.

Figure 3.1. Partisan strength in the House, 1964–2020

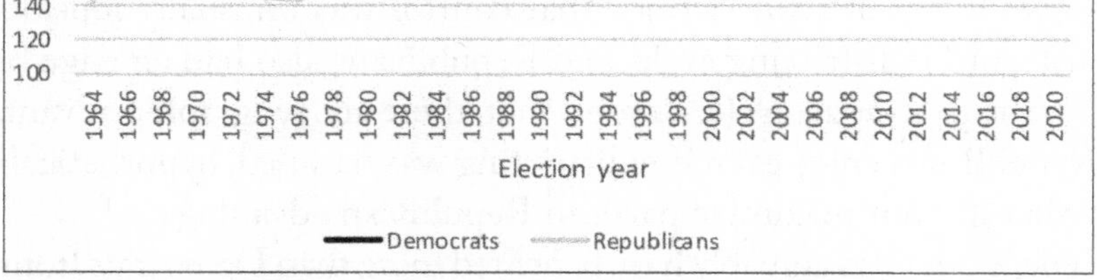

Source: Compiled by author

67

That said, the general trend over the past quarter century has been Republican control of the House.

Democrats won majorities in three national elections that broke decisively in their favor: the anti–George W. Bush/anti–Iraq War midterm of 2006, the anti–Donald Trump midterm of 2018 (when Democrats flipped the House from Republican control each time), and the general election victory of Barack Obama in 2008 (when they held the House). They also held the House in the more politically neutral though still Democratic-leaning environment of the 2020 presidential election. Republicans would win the House majority in every other election from 1996 to 2020, which includes years where the national House vote was narrowly divided (1996, 1998, and 2000) and even when the Democrats won slightly more House votes than Republicans (2012).

It may very well be that after decades of a dominating Democratic advantage in the House, there is now a persistent Republican edge. That's not to say that Democrats cannot win the majority—clearly, they can—but rather that one might expect a closely divided national battle for the House to break in favor of Republicans more often.

It's important to note that whatever advantages the Republicans currently hold in the US House of Representatives, they pale in comparison to the ones Democrats held for much of the 20th century. From 1930 through 1992, the average number of seats won by Democrats was 259, 41 seats higher than the majority threshold (218 seats).[1] From 1994 through 2020, the average number of seats won by the Republicans in each election was just 223 seats, or just 5 seats above the 218-seat threshold needed for the majority. The largest Republican majority in that timeframe, the 247 the party elected in 2014, is still considerably smaller than the six-decade Democratic average.

A review of recent literature on the House makes clear some of the reasons why Republicans may have an edge in the House: Republicans appear to have benefited from recent trends in House district line drawing over the past few decades, both because of the racial redistricting described in the previous chapter and also because of increasing GOP control of the state-level levers of redistricting. That control was unusually lopsided in the post-2010 redistricting cycle, and Republicans also had an edge heading into the post-2020 cycle. Beyond that, there are geographic advantages that Republicans enjoy even if redistricting was handled, hypothetically, in a way that did not maximize partisan Republican advantage.

Republicans also arguably have benefited more than Democrats from two big-picture trends in American politics: the declining power of incumbency and the increasing nationalization of election results, such that ticket splitting—voters in a given congressional district picking one party for president and the other party in their local House race—has become less common.

EVIDENCE FOR A PERSISTENT REPUBLICAN HOUSE EDGE

There is abundant evidence that the Republicans have enjoyed something of a structural advantage in the House over the last quarter century. There is, of course, the obvious: from 1995 to 2023, the Republicans will have held the majority about 70 percent of the time, while Democrats have only held it roughly 30 percent of the time. But beyond that, Republicans may be advantaged in that they may expect to win more than 50 percent of the seats when they win 50 percent of the national House vote. That used to be true for Democrats but is no longer the case.

House scholar Theodore S. Arrington finds that in both the 1970s and 1980s, Democrats could have expected to win 53.3 percent and 56.7 percent of the total seats if they won 50 percent of the two-party House vote. Arrington is able to compare results over time by estimating the vote totals in unopposed districts—the number of unopposed districts in a given year can have an impact on the raw national House votes—and excluding votes cast for third-party candidates. Arrington's adjusted House popular vote and seat share is displayed in figure 3.2.

Figure 3.2. Democratic share of the two-party adjusted House popular vote compared to share of seats won, 1972–2020

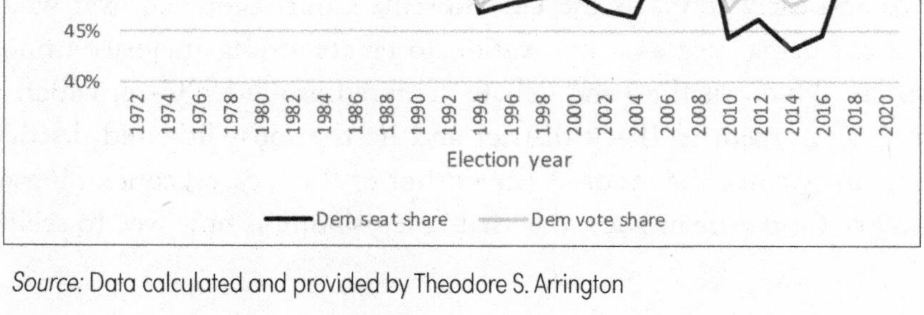

Source: Data calculated and provided by Theodore S. Arrington

However, by the 1990s Arrington finds that this Democratic advantage had eroded to the point where, during that decade, Democrats could only expect to win 50.3 percent of the seats with 50 percent of the vote, meaning that there wasn't much partisan bias one way or the other in the House that decade. In the 2000s and 2010s a Republican advantage appeared, such that Democrats could only expect to win 48.8 percent and 47.1 percent of the seats, respectively, with 50 percent of the vote.[2] However, Democrats overcame this seeming bias in both 2018 and 2020, winning roughly the same percentage of both the adjusted House vote and the percentage of House seats. In other words, there was a Republican bias in 2012, 2014, and 2016 but not in 2018 or 2020.

Redistricting analysts Nicholas Stephanopoulos and Eric McGhee created what they call the "efficiency gap" to determine whether congressional maps benefited one party or the other over the last several decades. In a nutshell, an efficiency gap in favor of one side means that one party can "claim more seats, relative to a zero-gap plan, *without claiming more votes.*"[3] Their findings, contra to Arrington, highlighted how neither party had much of an advantage in the 1970s, but they agreed with Arrington in finding an edge for Democrats in the 1980s. They then showed an increasing GOP edge in the 1990s to the 2000s and then into the 2010s.[4] Again, they differ with Arrington in some ways, but the overall takeaway is the same: as recently as the 1980s, the Democrats seemed to hold an advantage on the national House map. Yet now this advantage has shifted to Republicans.

Some of this probably has to do with the creation of majority-minority districts, covered at length in the last chapter. The Justice Department's push for such districts, which many experts believe helped Republicans pick up House seats in both 1992 and 1994, led to what legal scholar Samuel Issacharoff described as a "tortuous"[5] series of court decisions in the 1990s and early 2000s as the US Supreme Court agonized over what to do about using race as a motivation to create strong majority-minority districts. Much of the legal debate centered around NC-12, which was drawn as a majority Black district and is "the most litigated district in the country since the 1990s."[6] The upshot of these cases, concluding with *Easley v. Cromartie* in 2001, was that "a legislature is now free to seek any objective in redistricting, so long as it eschews any express commitment to providing representation to racial minorities," according to Issacharoff.[7] The snakelike NC-12 was only finally unraveled as part of a 2016 Republican partisan gerrymander forced by a racial redistricting court order.

In the process of this string of cases, several districts across many states drawn after the 1990 census as racial gerrymanders were thrown out and redrawn with smaller percentages of the minority group in question. However, political scientist Christian Grose finds that all of the Black members who ran for reelection in the same district with reduced Black populations ended up winning reelection anyway (although one, Cleo Fields of Louisiana, opted not to run after his district's Black population was reduced on two separate occasions).[8] The likeliest explanations for their victories were that these districts retained large-enough Black voting blocs (and in some instances remained majority-minority), as Grose demonstrates,[9] and also that the power of incumbency had helped them. Political scientists D. Stephen Voss and David Lublin provide evidence for both of these explanations in an analysis of the 1996 elections involving some Black incumbents whose districts were redrawn in response to Supreme Court intervention.[10]

More recently, Michael Li and Laura Royden of the liberal Brennan Center for Justice find that "majority-minority districts do not result in maps that unfairly favor either party" and that the creation of such districts "could, in fact, help reduce the high partisan bias in some of this decade's maps."[11]

Speaking of "high partisan bias," or the allegation thereof on the congressional maps drawn following the 2010 census, let's turn to the current state of partisan redistricting. If redistricting based on race was perhaps the primary focus of House districting literature in the 1990s and early 2000s, partisan redistricting is arguably the chief focus now.

Many scholars question the effectiveness of redistricting as a partisan weapon. Political scientist Mark Rush, writing in 1993, argued that the effect of partisan redistricting can be hard to measure. A major reason for this, Rush argued, is that unlike race (a classification a person carries for life), partisanship is not necessarily permanent. His analysis of voting behavior "undermines the assumption of consistent partisan behavior and thereby strikes at a fundamental assumption . . . that partisan constituencies—voting blocs—can be identified clearly, accurately, and easily."[12]

Writing around the same time, political scientists Andrew Gelman and Gary King made a positive argument for gerrymandering, or at least for redistricting: "Gerrymandering biases electoral systems in favor of the party that controls the redistricting as compared to what would have happened if the other party controlled it, but any type of redistricting reduces partisan bias as compared to an electoral system without redistricting."[13]

Even in an era defined by partisan polarization, voting preferences can and do swing wildly, particularly if a big surge for one party in the presidential contest is followed by a countersurge by the other party in the following midterm. This effect can cause significant changes in the performance of House candidates. Over the last four midterms (2006, 2010, 2014, and 2018), a study of US House results found that the presidential party candidate's share of the two-party vote declined by an average of 5.1 percentage points in these four midterms from the previous cycle's results.[14] This change in partisan swing can undo the designs of even the most skilled partisan mapmakers, turning a gerrymander into what political scientists Bernard Grofman and Thomas Brunell call the "dummymander," a "gerrymander by one party that, over the course of the decade, benefits the other party."[15] That dummymanders sometimes occur—Grofman and Brunell find several examples in the South after the 1990 and 2000 round of redistricting—lends credence to Rush's suggestion that a lack of "well-ordered and consistent voter preferences"[16] limits the power of partisan redistricting. However, the erosion of the Democrats' overall position in the South during the 1990s and 2000s also surely made it harder for southern Democrats to create sustainable partisan gerrymanders.

Political scientist Nicholas Seabrook finds that there are several legal and geographic constraints on redistricting and that partisan redistricting can actually increase competition in the long term, as opposed to bipartisan plans, where "both parties have incentives to reduce competitiveness, resulting in redistricting plans that carve out safe districts for incumbents of both political stripes."[17] He is not alone in this finding; for instance, House expert Thomas Mann finds that "a commission whose membership is evenly divided between the parties . . . is naturally drawn toward bipartisan compromise, which usually works to the advantage of incumbents and to the detriment of competition."[18] So to some scholars (specifically Seabrook), a potential cure for partisan redistricting—that is, engaging in bipartisan redistricting—may be worse than the disease itself.

Political scientists Anthony McGann, Charles Anthony Smith, Michael Latner, and Alex Keena find that "partisan bias increased sharply in the 2010 districting round"[19] and that the bias toward the Republicans was so large that the post-2010 GOP-dominated redistricting "has effectively determined control of the House of Representatives for a decade."[20] (The specifics of the GOP's post-2010 redistricting control are addressed in the history of the era that follows in this chapter.) The contention that the Democrats might have been prevented from winning the House until the next round of redistricting after the 2020 census was based in part on the fact that after the 2010 redistricting in the 2012 House election, Democrats won more House votes nationally than the Republicans but only captured 201 seats, 17 short of the 218 required for a majority. Sam Wang, a neuroscientist and electoral analyst, argues that Democrats would have needed to win the national House vote by seven points to win House control in 2012, and he attributes the Democratic roadblock to redistricting: "Politicians, especially Republicans facing demographic and ideological changes in the electorate, use redistricting to cling to power."[21] After Democrats took control of the presidency and both chambers of Congress following the 2020 election, the House passed a massive elections bill that included a mandate that all states use independent redistricting commissions to draw congressional districts. As of this writing, the Senate was considering the legislation, but it appeared unlikely to pass.[22] So just as Republicans, like then president George H. W. Bush, were frustrated by Democratic gerrymandering and favored federal intervention to place limits on the practice in the 1980s, Democrats are now seeking to do the same after Republicans acquired more gerrymandering power in the 21st century.

In any event, the suggestion that the post-2010 GOP gerrymanders made the House unwinnable for Democrats for the entirety of the following decade ended up being wrong, as Democrats won it fairly comfortably in 2018 and more narrowly in 2020. As noted in the election-by-election analysis later in this chapter, the unwinding of Republican gerrymanders throughout the course of the decade in Florida, North Carolina, Pennsylvania, and Virginia did help the Democrats over the course of the decade. But just because Democrats were capable of winning the House in 2018 and 2020 does not necessarily mean that the House does not have a Republican bias at this juncture of history.

According to political scientist Jonathan Rodden, there's one other wrinkle that may hurt the Democrats in the House. The Democrats have increasingly become an urban party, with the Republicans holding more rural areas, and the Democrats are hurt by this divide because, according to Rodden, "in many US states, Democrats are now concentrated in cities in such a way that even when districts are drawn without regard for partisanship, their seat share will fall well short of their vote share."[23] There is something compelling about this hypothesis that is borne out in district-level presidential results: in the 2020 presidential election, Democrat Joe Biden received 70 percent or more of the vote in 70 House districts, while Republican Donald Trump won 70 percent or more in just 26, according to figures calculated by Daily Kos Elections. Unsurprisingly, many of the Biden-won districts are majority-minority districts, demonstrating how the creation of such districts can create strongly Democratic seats given that voters of color are, collectively, a Democratic voting bloc. Biden carried roughly 70 percent of voters of color in 2020.[24]

McGann and colleagues take issue with the argument about geographic concentration, conceding that while the "urban concentration of the Democratic vote may make the drawing of pro-Republican partisan gerrymanders easier," they are not inevitable because the "bias of district plans, even in the most urbanized states, is a matter of political choice."[25]

Beyond partisan gerrymandering, there is the growing nationalization of politics. Political scientists Alan Abramowitz and Steven Webster note that "recent elections in the United States have been characterized by the highest levels of party loyalty and straight-ticket voting since the American National Election Studies first began measuring party identification in 1952" and that there is "a growing connection between the results of presidential elections and the results of House, Senate and even state legislative elections."[26] Following the 2018 election, Abramowitz also reiterated his findings that House elections were becoming more nationalized and that ideological moderation was no longer much of an electoral reward for incumbents.[27]

House expert Gary Jacobson found in 2015 that the electoral advantage of incumbency for House members had been in decline. Incumbency throughout much of the 1960s to the 2000s meant getting a boost, generally speaking, in the high single digits; however, by the 2010s, the advantage had dipped to just three or four points: "The incumbency advantage has diminished in conjunction with an increase in party loyalty, straight-ticket voting, and president-centered electoral nationalization, products of the widening and increasingly coherent partisan divisions in the American electorate. Consequently, House incumbents now have a much harder time retaining districts that lean toward the rival party," Jacobson wrote.[28] In 2018, the incumbency advantage was less than two points, Jacobson found, which was the smallest edge since the 1950s.[29] However, political scientist Jeffrey Stonecash finds that the average vote for all incumbents from 1946 through 2014 was effectively flat. His calculation is unique because he includes uncontested incumbents in his calculation, whereas Jacobson and others exclude uncontested races.[30]

Republicans arguably benefit from a nationalized electoral environment where the skew of the House map meant a meager incumbency advantage. If incumbents are only running slightly ahead of the partisan lean of their districts, Republicans are at an advantage because the median House seat has a pro-Republican bias.

Even after middecade redistricting helped Democrats in a handful of states in the second half of the 2010s, the median House seat by 2016 presidential results, Rep. Mario Diaz-Balart's (R) South Florida–based FL-25, voted for Donald Trump by about two points while Hillary Clinton won the national popular vote by two points. So the median House seat was about four points to the right of the nation. In 2020 the median seat by presidential performance was Rep. Lauren Underwood's (D) Chicago-area IL-14, which Joe Biden won by 2.4 points, or about two points worse than Biden's 4.5-point national win. So the Republican bias was smaller, but it was still present (and the national House map was more advantageous for Democrats in 2020 than it was in 2016 because

Democrats won better maps in North Carolina and Pennsylvania through state court orders).

If we expect presidential and House results to remain in alignment, and the median House seat votes to the right of the nation in presidential elections, that certainly is suggestive of a political playing field in which one would rather be a Republican, tactically speaking, in the race for the House. Generally that has been the case in the post-1994 era, although not always.

Overall, there was considerable disagreement about the importance of gerrymandering to political outcomes, but political scientists John Sides and Eric McGhee take a reasonable middle view (a view shared by this author). On one hand, say Sides and McGhee, "gerrymanders will likely be more effective in the future because the partisanship of a district, independent of incumbency or any other factors, is a more important predictor of House elections than it was several decades ago." On the other hand, they offer a caveat: "There is a lot more than redistricting to House elections. Democrats are concentrated in urban areas. Incumbents still outperform their party's presidential candidate. And the electorate can still change its mind, as the turmoil of the last decade has made clear."[31] The history of House elections in the post–Reapportionment Revolution era is dotted with many successful partisan gerrymanders, as described in previous chapters and discussed later in this chapter. But there are also gerrymandered maps that don't perform the way the partisans who drew them intended, either in the first election after they were implemented or in elections to follow. That said, the frequency of out-and-out partisan gerrymandering failures described in previous chapters—like those by New York Republicans in the early 1970s, Indiana Republicans in the 1980s, and Georgia Democrats in the 1990s, among others—seems to be decreasing. While maps do not always perform the way partisan gerrymanderers intend, the stronger partisanship and weaker incumbency of this era likely make these partisan maps more foolproof than they once were, as Sides and McGhee suggest.

Immediately following the Republican takeover in 1994, the House was closely contested, but there were no big swings in seat totals from year to year. But that changed in 2006, when the Democrats took over, and the

House has continued to feature big swings at regular intervals, with the biggest ones coming in midterm elections.

1996: REGIONAL DIVIDES KEEP REPUBLICANS AHEAD

House elected: 227–208 Republican
Change from previous election: +3 Democratic

Two years after the Republican Revolution, the GOP tried to do something it hadn't done since before the New Deal: reelect a previously held House majority. Republicans succeeded in that task and only lost 3 net seats—in other words, they suffered hardly any overall backslide from their monumental 54-seat gain in 1994. However, the regional disparities in the results were telling.

In the Northeast, Midwest, and on the West Coast, Democrats made major gains in the House, netting 15 seats across the three regions in the midst of President Bill Clinton's impressive 8.5-point reelection victory over the former Senate majority leader, Bob Dole, who resigned earlier in 1996 to focus on his presidential campaign. Democrats actually narrowly won a majority of the seats in the Midwest, something the party sometimes failed to do when it otherwise held House majorities in previous decades. Had the Democrats simply held the seats won in 1994 in the Greater South and Interior West, they would have regained a narrow majority. However, Republicans netted an additional dozen seats in these two generally conservative regions in 1996, which protected their majority.

Most of these Republican gains came in the South, which was further aligning its historic conservatism with the GOP. The realignment was continuing and keeping Republicans ahead. In Alabama, Republicans picked up two open seats, the Third and Fourth Districts, which had been carried by both 1996 GOP presidential nominee Bob Dole and George H. W. Bush four years earlier.

The realignment was quite literal for three southern Democrats: Reps. Nathan Deal (GA-9), Billy Tauzin (LA-3), and Mike Parker (MS-4) all switched from Democratic to Republican in advance of the 1996 election and easily won reelection under their new party banner. Another southern Democratic defector, Rep. Greg Laughlin (TX-14), lost his primary, but his Dole-Bush district would stay Republican. In the primary he was beaten by Ron Paul, who had previously served in the House; Paul would go on to run as a Libertarian-influenced Republican presidential candidate in 2008 and 2012 (after having been the official Libertarian presidential nominee in 1988).

In the Interior West, Rick Hill (R, MT-AL) and John Thune (R, SD-AL) won their sparsely populated, Dole-voting statewide districts as Democrats failed to defend these open seats, and Chris Cannon (R) beat Rep. Bill Orton (D, UT-3) in a district Dole carried by 29 points.

Not all of the Republicans' southern gains came on clearly Republican turf. In a Louisville-based seat, state representative Anne Northup (R) narrowly defeated first-term representative Mike Ward (D, KY-3), himself an extremely close winner in 1994. "In a year when almost all Democrats and most Republicans ran cookie-cutter identical campaigns, Northup showed originality in strategy and tactics," outraising Ward and attacking him over his vote against a bill to make English the nation's official language, observed Michael Barone and Grant Ujifusa in the 1998 *Almanac of American Politics*. Northup also criticized the tobacco industry, showing independence in a state where the industry was powerful.[32] She won in a district Clinton carried by 13 points. She would run ahead of the Democratic tide in her district for a decade before losing in the 2006 Democratic wave.

Redistricting also played a limited role. In Louisiana, the Supreme Court unwound the state's districts as constituting an illegal racial gerrymander. Rep. Cleo Fields (D, LA-5) saw the Black percentage of his district slashed dramatically and decided not to run again; a Republican replaced him. However, two Black Democrats in Georgia won reelection despite a new map that reduced the Black percentages in their districts. A remap in Texas did not really have an impact on the results, where Republicans netted a total of two seats as Paul won, and two other Republicans flipped open seats. Democrats flipped one seat in the Lone Star State as Nick Lampson (D) beat first-term representative Steve Stockman (R, TX-9) in a competitive district; Stockman had defeated long-serving representative Jack Brooks (D) in 1994.

Lampson's win was indicative of many Democratic takeovers in 1996, as Democrats reclaimed seats lost two years earlier during the Republican Revolution. Nine other Democrats won back seats in such a fashion, including David Price (D, NC-4) and Ted Strickland (D, OH-6), who both beat the Republican candidates who had defeated them two years earlier. Rod Blagojevich (D, IL-5) reclaimed the heavily Democratic seat that disgraced House leader Dan Rostenkowski had lost two years earlier; Blagojevich would later become governor of Illinois and, like Rostenkowski, ultimately end up in jail over corruption.

All told, Clinton had won 9 of these 10 districts that Democrats reclaimed. The one exception to this Clinton-district trend was Bob Etheridge (D), who beat Rep. David Funderburk (R, NC-2) in a district Dole won by 10 points. But there were extenuating circumstances: Funderburk and his wife were involved in an automobile accident in which witnesses indicated Funderburk was driving but then left the scene and returned with his wife behind the wheel, dealing his reelection campaign what was probably a lethal blow.[33]

A few other districts won by Democrats were ones they had lost in 1992 but that Clinton won by double digits in 1996; one, on Cleveland's West Side, was recaptured by Dennis Kucinich (D, OH-10), who would later achieve national notoriety as a gadfly Democratic presidential candidate. The two others were in Massachusetts; since 1996, Democrats have won every single House election held in this heavily Democratic state.

Overall, the 1996 election featured countervailing trends that were defined to no small degree by presidential partisanship. Given that the Republicans had surged to their first majority in four decades by netting 54 seats in 1994, their net loss of just 3 seats represented a strong overall outcome in the midst of an impressive reelection victory by the other party's president.

1998–2000: The GOP Loses Ground (but Only Slightly)

House elected (1998): 223–212 Republican
Change from previous election: +4 Democratic
House elected (2000): 222–213 Republican
Change from previous election: +1 Democratic

Much of the lead-up to the 1998 midterm was dominated by the travails of President Clinton, whose affair with a White House intern, Monica

Lewinsky, threatened his presidency even as he enjoyed high approval ratings and in a time of peace and prosperity.[34]

Clinton biographer Michael Tomasky sums up the premidterm thinking this way: "It was expected that the Republicans would augment their majorities, and probably by a considerable amount. Rarely in politics had anything been so obvious."[35] That assessment was informed by history: this was a so-called sixth-year-itch election, a midterm conducted during a second consecutive term of a party's control of the White House. There were some catastrophically bad sixth-year-itch elections in recent memory: 1938, 1958, 1966, and 1974 all qualified (later, 2006 and perhaps 2014 would as well). The president's party in each of those years was undone by overreach, scandal, war, recession, or some combination of those factors. For Republicans, the hope was that the scandal that would deliver them victory was Clinton's dalliance with Lewinsky, which he denied under oath, providing fodder for the Republicans' efforts to impeach and remove him from office.

And yet in many ways Republicans were not set up for significant gains in 1998. Democrats had only made a minor gain in 1996, so they did not hold many newly vulnerable seats, and Democrats had lost many of their most vulnerable seats in the previous two cycles. Following his comfortable reelection victory in 1996, Clinton's approval rating was consistently strong throughout 1997 and 1998, even as he would deal with personal scandal. He spent 1997 enjoying approval ratings mostly in the high 50s, according to FiveThirtyEight's historical average,[36] and in 1998 his approval was in the 60s, even after reports of his affair emerged in January 1998. The economy was strong, and the nation was at peace. These are not the sort of conditions that suggested a Republican wave. But Republicans had high expectations anyway: "Gingrich spent the fall boasting that he foresaw his Republicans gaining as many as forty House seats," writes Tomasky.[37]

This was probably unrealistic almost in any event, and the Democrats actually gained four seats. For the first time since 1934, the president's party had actually netted seats in a midterm election. There is at least some anecdotal evidence from certain campaigns that the push for impeachment contributed to the Republicans' poor overall result.

In NJ-12, first-term representative Mike Pappas (R) recited a poem on the House floor paying tribute to the polarizing independent counsel who investigated Clinton: "Twinkle twinkle, Kenneth Starr, now we see how brave you are. We could not see which way to go, if you did not lead us so."[38] Rush Holt (D) put the clip in campaign ads and eked out a three-point victory. Impeachment may have made the difference, although Pappas had only won by three points himself in 1996 in a district Clinton had carried by six. Jay Inslee (D), who later was elected to three terms as Washington State's governor, was in 1998 a former House member who had lost in the 1994 GOP wave. He ran in a more Democratic district than the one he had lost four years before and beat Rep. Rick White (R, WA-1), who himself had beaten another familiar name from Washington politics, Rep. (now Sen.) Maria Cantwell (D), in 1994. Inslee ran ads arguing that "Rick White and Newt Gingrich shouldn't be dragging us through this."[39] In suburban Philadelphia's PA-13, Joe Hoeffel (D) reclaimed another Clinton-won district four years after former representative Marjorie Margolies-Mezvinsky (D) lost it to Jon Fox (R) in the wake of her famous and decisive vote for Clinton's 1993 budget and tax increase. Hoeffel stayed away from Clinton but did have First Lady Hillary Clinton campaign for him.[40] Despite the above examples, House Democratic candidates generally did not run ads on impeachment; one who did, Chris Gorman (D), narrowly lost to Anne Northup (R, KY-3) in her Louisville-based seat.[41] Gingrich, who resigned after the election, helped orchestrate a late-October advertising blitz of key House districts focused on Clinton's relationship with Lewinsky. This was probably a miscalculation.[42]

Impeachment did allow some Democrats to break with the national party: for instance, Rep. James Maloney (D, CT-5), who was damaged by campaign finance problems, voted for the GOP motion to hold impeachment hearings. He won a narrow victory.[43] Democrats also benefited from some key Republican retirements, such as that of moderate representative Scott Klug (R, WI-2) in a district based around liberal Madison. Clinton had won the district by 22 points in 1996; Tammy Baldwin (D), later elected in 2012 to the Senate, would flip the seat in 1998. House elections did not follow presidential voting as closely then as they do now, but part of the 1998 story was Democratic districts like WI-2 coming into line with their presidential partisanship. Democrats also were able to hold some difficult open seats, like IN-9, where Rep. Lee Hamilton (D) had retired and where neither the Democratic nor Republican candidate emphasized impeachment.[44]

Overall, only 17 races in 1998 were decided by five points or less. The Democrats won 10 and the Republicans 7. Perhaps in the absence of impeachment, the GOP would have won the majority of the closer races and could've netted seats instead of losing a small number. But even without the impeachment factor, the Republicans would probably not have performed significantly better than they did.

The 1998 results pushed the Democrats somewhat closer to the majority, setting up a battle for control amidst the 2000 presidential election, one of the closest in American history. As it was, Vice President Al Gore (D) would win the national popular vote by about half a percentage point, but Gov. George W. Bush (R-TX), whose father was the most recent Republican president, narrowly prevailed in the Electoral College. The House results reflected the close presidential race, but the Republicans kept the majority.

The nationalization trend continued. For the first time since the 1952 election, fewer than 100 House seats (only 86 total) voted for different parties for president and for House. Many of the Democratic gains came in California, where they picked up four seats. Gore actually ran ahead of Clinton's 1996 margin in all four districts, an unmistakable sign of a Democratic trend that was bleeding down the ballot (remember, Gore's national margin was eight percentage points below Clinton's, meaning these districts became much more Democratic relative to the rest of the country in 2000 than they had been in 1996). All told, in 2000 Democrats would set what was then a high-water mark for the party in the state: 32 out of 52 seats in total.

Reps. Ron Klink (D, PA-4) and Rick Lazio (R, NY-2) left their seats to pursue unsuccessful Senate bids against, respectively, future presidential aspirants Rick Santorum (R) and outgoing first lady Clinton. They were replaced by Melissa Hart (R) and Steve Israel (D), matching up the party affiliation of the districts with their presidential winners.

Still, not every seat corresponded to national partisanship. In eastern Connecticut, Rob Simmons (R) upset the 20-year incumbent, Rep. Sam Gejdenson (D, CT-2), in part because of the longtime incumbent's residency issues, which compounded other baggage he had amassed over a long career.[45] But the Northeast remained a Democratic bastion, as the party retained control of roughly 60 percent of the seats in the region. In northeast Oklahoma, attorney Brad Carson (D, OK-2) won a Clinton-to-Bush open seat. Jim Matheson (D), the son of a popular former governor, overcame Bush's 23-point victory to flip, by 15 points, the Salt Lake City–based UT-2 after the Republican incumbent, Merrill Cook, lost his primary amidst reports of "temper tantrums [and] staff turnover."[46]

A rural trend toward George W. Bush helped doom Rep. David Minge (D, MN-2), who lost to Mark Kennedy in southwest Minnesota in a squeaker as the district swung from Clinton by 6 to Bush by 14. Retiring representative Pat Danner (D, MO-6) tried to hand off her sprawling northwest Missouri district to her son, a state senator, but another state senator, Sam Graves (R), rode a presidential shift from Clinton by four to Bush by nine to victory.

West Virginia, which in 1980 and 1988 had been so pro-Democratic in presidential elections that it backed Democratic presidential candidates in the midst of significant Republican national victories, flipped to George W. Bush in 2000 as part of this broader trend. A 19-point swing from Clinton (by 9) to Bush (by 10) helped Shelley Moore Capito (R, WV-2), daughter of a former governor, win an open seat stretching across the central part of the state. She was the first Republican to win a House race in the Mountain State in 18 years; later, in 2014, she would become the first Republican to win a Senate race in West Virginia since 1956.

All told, there was hardly any net change: Democrats netted a seat, which could have been two had conservative representative Virgil Goode (I, VA-5) not left the party and joined the GOP caucus. Still, with Bush in the White House, and needing just five net seats to retake the House in the 2002 midterm, the Democrats on paper seemed like they might be well positioned for victory. But it didn't work out that way.

2002–4: The Republicans Extend Their Edge amidst Reapportionment, War

House elected (2002): 229–206 Republican
Change from previous election: +7 Republican
House elected (2004): 232–203 Republican
Change from previous election: +3 Republican

For the second straight midterm—but for only the third time since the Civil War—the president's party netted House seats, this time under George W. Bush. This was an unusual midterm, contested in the shadow of the devastating September 11, 2001, terrorist attacks on New York City and Washington, DC, and in the run-up to war in Iraq launched in early 2003. Bush "set a new precedent" as a midterm presidential campaigner, barnstorming the country in support of Republican candidates.[47] The president, whose approval ratings were in the 60s throughout the fall campaign, was clearly an asset.[48] But the Republicans had other advantages in the 2002 battle for the House. Namely, they had a much stronger hand in redistricting than they were accustomed to.

Even though the 1992 reapportionment and redistricting round ended up benefiting Republicans thanks in part to the George H. W. Bush administration's push for majority-minority districts, Republicans didn't really have much true gerrymandering power that year: they only had direct control over the drawing of a minuscule 5 districts out of 435.[49] But in 2002, they had significantly more control: Democrats still had total control over the drawing of districts in 135 seats, but Republicans had similar power in 98 seats. The remainder were in at-large states or ones where neither party could exercise total control because of divided government or some sort of specified bipartisan or nonpartisan process.[50] The places where the GOP held redistricting sway included several populous, competitive states: Florida, Michigan, Ohio, and Pennsylvania. Republicans would use that power to significant effect.

Compounding the Democratic challenge is that many of the states where Democrats retained redistricting control were in the South, which was becoming increasingly Republican. For instance, Alabama Democrats attempted to improve their party's position, but they failed to make a dent in the GOP's five-to-two control of the delegation.[51] Georgia Democrats drew a gerrymander intended to allow the party to win two new seats the state had gained in reapportionment, but they ended up winning only one of them.[52] They did also pick up another district, but their plan to push out Rep. Saxby Chambliss (R) prompted him to run for Senate, and he beat Sen. Max Cleland (D-GA) in a bitter race.

Something similar happened in Maryland. The Democratic gerrymander allowed the party to pick up two seats: Chris Van Hollen (D) beat Rep. Constance Morella (R, MD-8), a moderate in the otherwise very Democratic Washington, DC, suburbs, and Dutch Ruppersberger (D) won a redrawn Baltimore-area seat designed to eliminate Rep. Bob Ehrlich (R, MD-2). However, Ehrlich ended up running for governor and, to the dismay of Democrats, he won.

The Republican gerrymanders were cleaner. In Florida, the GOP picked up the two new seats the state had won in reapportionment and also altered Rep. Karen Thurman's (D, FL-5) district, helping state senator Ginny Brown-Waite (R) narrowly defeat her in "an election decided by redistricting."[53] Republican redistricters eliminated Democratic seats in states that lost ground in reapportionment, lopping off one seat apiece in Michigan and Ohio and two in Pennsylvania, and they otherwise gained ground in all three states thanks to redistricting handiwork.

Other states would effectively protect incumbents. In California, a new map gave the Democrats the extra seat the Golden State had won in reapportionment. For the rest of the decade, of 265 individual House elections for 53 districts held from 2002 to 2010, only a single seat switched hands: Jerry McNerney (D) beat Rep. Richard Pombo (R, CA-11) as part of the Democrats' 2006 wave. Otherwise, the state's map was static.

All told, in states that lost districts because of reapportionment, Democrats lost nine seats, while Republicans lost just three (some of these losses included races in which a Democrat and a Republican were forced into the same district, and the losing party is included as the loser in this tally). The states that lost seats were mostly in the Northeast and Midwest, which has been the usual pattern for decades, with exceptions coming in Mississippi and Oklahoma.

Those 12 seats went to states in the West and South. Of those 12 new seats, Republicans won 8, and Democrats won 4. That nets out to a 5-seat gain for Republicans from the shift in seats, which almost entirely accounted for their 7-seat net gain in 2002. However, 3 of the GOP's gains from the creation of new seats were in marginal districts: AZ-1, CO-7, and NV-3. While the Republicans won these seats in 2002, they would eventually lose them in tougher cycles later in the decade.

Had Bush been a liability in 2002 instead of an asset, Republicans might have lost the House anyway. But the combination of redistricting and reapportionment protected against a Democratic comeback, and Bush and the national political environment took care of the rest. Republicans now held a 229–206 majority, essentially the same as their 230–205 majority won in the 1994 breakthrough. The incremental Democratic progress of 1996, 1998, and 2000 had been largely reversed.

The sorting out of the parties in the House continued apace. The combination of reapportionment, redistricting, and the 2002 results further reduced the number of crossover districts, those carried by different parties for president in 2000 and House in 2002. There were 46 Democrats who carried Bush-won seats and 40 Republicans who carried Gore-won seats in 2000; by 2002, there were just 32 Bush-district Democrats and 26 Gore-district Republicans.[54]

As the calendar turned to 2003, the Democrats' prospects of winning the House took another major blow, thanks to momentous developments in a state that in the 2000 reapportionment passed New York with the nation's second-largest House delegation: Texas.

The Lone Star State was continuing its turn toward the Republicans. While it hadn't voted for a Democratic presidential candidate since 1976, George W. Bush's candidacy took the state to a different GOP level in 2000: He won the state, where he was the sitting governor, by 21 points, pushing Texas to its biggest Republican presidential lean relative to the nation in the state's history. Two years later, Rick Perry (R), who as the lieutenant governor had taken over for Bush after he became president, won the governorship by 18 points, and Republicans won a coveted majority in the state's House of Representatives. The GOP had previously won the state senate, so the Republicans now had a "trifecta" and unified control of state government. As part of this sweep, Republicans won the state's overall US House vote by nine points in 2002. And yet Democrats retained a majority of the state's House delegation, 17–15. Republicans picked up the state's two new seats, but otherwise a court-drawn map, created after the then-divided state government stalemated on a plan, effectively gave "new life" to the Democratic gerrymander from a decade prior.[55]

The Republicans' new power in state government allowed them to draw a new map. Even though almost all states redistrict only once a decade in response to the census (unless a court steps in to order new lines), nothing in federal law technically prevents a state from redrawing its House districts any time it likes. So Texas Republicans pushed through a gerrymander that would devastate the Democrats. Democratic state lawmakers fled the state twice as a way to deny majority Republicans a quorum to pass this bill, but the GOP persisted and imposed the new map.[56]

It worked. In 2004, the GOP turned a 17–15 disadvantage in the state delegation into a 21–11 edge, netting six seats; that included another party switcher, Rep. Ralph Hall (R, TX-4), giving GOP representation to the district that was the descendant of the one held by legendary former Speaker of the House Sam Rayburn (D). Given the trends toward nationalization, it may have been that Republicans would have broken through in the 2000s even on the old map: six Texas Democrats (including Hall) held seats that Bush had won by double digits. But the middecade remap meant that the Republicans didn't have to deal with that hypothetical.

As Bush won a second term as president in a close battle with Sen. John Kerry (D-MA), Democrats actually netted three House seats in the 49 states outside Texas. But the six-seat net gain in Texas pushed the Republicans to a 232–203 majority, slightly bigger than the one they had captured in the 1994 wave.

Overall, just 58 districts would vote for different parties for president and for House, setting another new record in the post–World War II era.

2006 AND 2008: BUSH BACKLASH, OBAMA WAVE REOPEN DEMO-CRATIC OPPORTUNITIES ON CONSERVATIVE TURF

House elected (2006): 233–202 Democratic
Change from previous election: +30 Democratic
House elected (2008): 257–178 Democratic
Change from previous election: +24 Democratic

Following his reelection, George W. Bush and the Republicans made a number of significant missteps. In 2005 Bush pushed for changes to Social Security that would allow Americans to invest the payroll taxes they paid into it (opponents called this a privatization plan). "Observers noticed that the more the President talked about Social Security, the more support for his plan declined," journalist William Galston noted in a postmortem.[57] The plan was dying over the summer, and the government's weak response to the devastation wrought by Hurricane Katrina in New Orleans and the broader Gulf Coast diverted the public's attention. Bush, who had become a polarizing figure over the Iraq War—which was becoming increasingly unpopular during (and especially after) his bitterly contested reelection— saw his approval rating plummet throughout the second half of 2005.[58] By the end of the year, Bush's approval according to Gallup was 43 percent, while his disapproval was 53 percent. The conditions were emerging for a big midterm backlash against the president—a scenario that had not oc-curred often over the preceding few decades but was common in troubled times and under unpopular presidents.

Perhaps hidden in the 2004 results was the Democrats' ability to win districts that on paper did not make much sense for them to hold due to growing nationalization of down-ballot results. In a pair of special elec-tions held in the first half of 2004, Ben Chandler (D, KY-6) and Stephanie Herseth (D, SD-AL) picked up a couple of previously Republican-held seats in districts that Bush had won (and would win in 2004) by double digits. Chandler and Herseth both held on in the regularly scheduled elections in the fall. They were 2 of the 40 Democrats who won Bush districts in 2004; only 18 Republicans won Kerry seats. That Democrats remained at a fairly significant disadvantage in the House despite attract-ing significantly more crossover support was, on one hand, an ominous sign. On the other hand, it also meant that the party was figuring out ways to generate such backing in Bush-won turf by producing appealing candidates who could create some distance between themselves and the more liberal national party. Creating such distance was made easier by the Democrats being locked out of power in Washington: it is easier to distance oneself from the national party when the national party does not have the ability to advance its preferred liberal policy. During her general election campaign in 2004, Herseth—who would later go by Stephanie Herseth Sandlin after marrying former representative Max Sandlin (D), one of the casualties of the Texas GOP gerrymander—was pressed by her opponent on how she would cast the South Dakota House delegation's vote for president in the event that an Electoral College tie would be broken by the US House of Representatives (because each state gets just one vote in such a scenario and because Herseth Sandlin would be the only member of the state's single-seat delegation, she would have total control over how to cast the state's vote). She said she would back Bush because Bush would, of course, win the state.[59]

Democratic Congressional Campaign Committee chairman Rahm Emanuel (D, IL-5), who had won Dan Rostenkowski's old Chicago seat after Rod Blagojevich won the Illinois governorship in 2002, decided "to seriously contest districts which on the basis of 2004 figures were not winnable."[60] One of Emanuel's top recruits was former NFL quarterback Heath Shuler, who would go on to defeat Rep. Charles Taylor (R, NC-11) in a western North Carolina seat. "An evangelical Christian who opposes abortion, Shuler couldn't easily have his views caricatured by the GOP," the *Chicago Tribune*'s Naftali Bendavid observed in an Emanuel profile after the election.[61]

"One of the advantages the out party usually has is that its candidates are free to adapt to local terrain," Michael Barone wrote in his introductory essay to the 2008 *Almanac of American Politics.* "Democrats in 2006 ran successfully as moderates or even conservatives in Indiana, North Carolina, Texas and Arizona. They were also able to run as full-throated Bush and Iraq war opponents in Connecticut and suburban Pennsylvania, New Hampshire and Upstate New York," he added.[62] The 2006 Democratic House majority would resemble the old pre-1994 Democratic House majorities, which had featured a push and pull between liberal and conservative members.

However, this also would be a different kind of Democratic House majority than any in the history of the long-standing Democratic versus Republican two-party duality. The Democrats had won a healthy majority in 2006 despite winning just 41 percent of the seats in the Greater South; even in 1994, when the GOP won the House, the Democrats still held 48 percent of the seats in that region. Meanwhile, the Democratic coalition was pulling more and more of its members from the increasingly Democratic Northeast and West Coast. In 1994 the 68-member West Coast delegation was split 34–34, and the Northeast only had a modest 52–45 Democratic edge. By 2006, the Democrats had expanded this 7-seat net edge in these two regions to an astounding 67 seats. As part of this, the Democrats almost completely wiped out Republicans in New England: they picked up both seats in New Hampshire after Republicans had held them uninterrupted since 1994, and they also knocked off two Kerry-district Republicans in Connecticut, leaving moderate representative Chris Shays (R, CT-5) as the only Republican House member from the six states of New England. Shays was one of a number of surprise GOP swing district survivors in 2006: others included Reps. Heather Wilson (R, NM-1), Deborah Pryce (R, OH-15), and Jim Gerlach (R, PA-6).

The Interior West retained its GOP edge, and the Democrats once again won a House majority without a majority in the still highly competitive Midwest, where Republicans maintained a slender 46–45 edge even after losing eight net seats.

House analyst David Wasserman identified several reasons for the Democratic takeover.[63] One was scandal. Powerful House majority leader Tom DeLay (R, TX-22), arguably the mastermind of the Texas redistricting power play, resigned before the election after facing a campaign finance charge, leaving a write-in candidate to attempt to unsuccessfully defend his safe (on paper, at least) Republican district. So, too, did Reps. Bob Ney (R, OH-18) and Mark Foley (R, FL-16), the latter over a scandal in which Foley was found to have "exchanged sexually explicit instant messages with under-age male House pages."[64] Rep. Don Sherwood (R, PA-10) remained on the ballot but struggled with accusations that he had choked his mistress; he lost to Chris Carney (D) in a GOP-leaning northeast Pennsylvania district.[65] Democrats would net four seats in the Keystone State alone as the state's GOP-drawn map broke under the strain of the Democratic wave, turning a gerrymander into a dummymander. Democrats also clawed back a seat in Texas thanks to court-ordered modifications to the GOP gerrymander from 2004: Ciro Rodriguez (D) beat Rep. Henry Bonilla (R, TX-23) in a December 2006 runoff. It was an improbable comeback for Rodriguez, a former member who had lost a primary to Henry Cuellar (D) in TX-28 in 2004 and then lost to Cuellar again in 2006 before beating Bonilla in the redistricting-necessitated runoff.

Just as Texas Republicans had done when they took control of that state after the 2002 elections, Georgia Republicans attempted their own middecade remap after taking control of state government in 2004. However, the Georgia Republicans did not act in as much of a cutthroat manner as their Texas colleagues, as their primary goal was to shore up Rep. Phil Gingrey (R, GA-11), who had won in 2002 and 2004 a district gerrymandered to elect a Democrat. Republicans did weaken Reps. Jim Marshall (D, GA-8) and John Barrow (D, GA-12), but not by enough, as they survived challenges from former Republican House members in districts Bush had won two years prior. (Marshall would end up losing in the GOP wave year of 2010, though.)[66]

Democrats would net 30 seats overall, flipping the 232–203 GOP edge into almost an exact mirror opposite 233–202 Democratic majority. House Democratic leader Nancy Pelosi (D, CA-8) became the first woman to serve as Speaker of the House. The number of total "crossover" members expanded in the Democrats' favor: just 8 Republicans in Kerry-won districts survived, while Democrats elected 62 members from districts Bush had won.[67]

The 2006 and 2008 elections can, in effect, be lumped together as a rolling wave against the Republicans. Bush remained dreadfully unpopular, and the twin crises of the lingering Iraq War and a September 2008 financial crisis left the GOP at a major national disadvantage. Sen. Barack Obama (D-IL) would defeat Sen. Hillary Clinton (D-NY) in an epic 2008 Democratic presidential primary and vanquish Sen. John McCain (R-AZ), the GOP nominee, by seven points in November, becoming the first-ever Black president. Democrats would net another 24 seats in the 2008 cycle, meaning that they had netted 54 seats over two cycles, matching the GOP gain from 1994. Their 257-seat caucus was nearly as large as their 259-seat membership won in 1992—but that was a year in which Democrats lost 9 net seats. So it took two great performances in a row (2006 and 2008) to effectively replicate what in 1992 was an average-sized pre-GOP-takeover Democratic House majority.

Some of the Democratic gains in 2008 essentially represented unfinished business from 2006. Chris Shays, the lone New England Republican, couldn't hold on in 2008. Deborah Pryce, the suburban Columbus Republican who narrowly won in 2006, retired, allowing 2006 challenger Mary Jo Kilroy (D) to capture the open seat. Another 2006 survivor, Heather Wilson, lost a Senate primary, allowing Martin Heinrich (D) to win her Albuquerque-based seat. All told, Democrats picked up 12 open seats while Republicans didn't flip a single one. Republicans did claw back a couple of the seats they arguably had no business losing in 2006, such as the seats formerly held by Foley and DeLay two years earlier. But Democrats replaced those by winning a couple of heavily Republican southern districts with conservative candidates, AL-2 and MS-1—the latter won by Travis Childers (D) in an early 2008 special election that he then held in the fall.

Speaking of special elections, Democrats flipped another seat in early 2008: IL-14, a double-digit Bush seat that the former House Speaker, Dennis Hastert (R), left behind when he resigned (it would flip to Obama in 2008 as the presence of the Democratic-trending state's home-state senator on the ballot hypercharged Illinois's blue turn). Another Republican gerrymander from earlier in the decade fell apart under the Obama wave: in Ohio, Democrats netted four seats (the open seat won by Kilroy and three others) to take a 10–8 statewide majority in the delegation. They also picked up three seats in New York, taking a 26–3 majority in that state's delegation. The number of crossover districts had ballooned to 83, but part of this was the size of Obama's victory, which was significantly larger than Bush's narrow victories in 2000 and 2004 (a president who wins by a wider margin will naturally carry more districts than a closer winner).

The Democrats now had unified control of the federal government for the first time since 1993–94. That trifecta ended in the crushing defeat of 1994. Democrats in 2009–10 would enjoy more policy victories than they did in that earlier period of power. They also would suffer an even bigger midterm defeat.

2010: The Republican Revolt

House elected: 242–193 Republican
Change from previous election: +64 Republican

On paper, the Democrats in 2009 did not necessarily seem much more overextended than the Republicans. Yes, they held 49 districts carried by McCain in 2008, but Republicans held 34 won by Obama. And Democrats seemed to be on the verge of a new golden age. Stuart Rothenberg, one of the nation's top political handicappers, summed up the popular thinking in an April 2009 column: "The chance of Republicans winning control of either chamber in the 2010 midterm elections is zero."[68]

But in truth, the Democrats *were* significantly overextended. Of those 49 McCain-won seats they were defending, almost half (24) were districts Obama had lost by double digits. In fact, Democrats actually carried 31 of Obama's 150 worst-performing districts in 2008.[69] The 34 Obama-won Republicans were in much more marginal districts; just 9 were ones Obama had carried by double digits.

And now that Democrats were in charge, they would have to govern. In response to a massive recession prompted by the financial crisis that had helped Obama get elected, the Democrats passed an expensive fiscal stimulus bill with very little support from Republicans. The GOP, deep in the minority, was not inclined to give Democrats any bipartisan cover, and the backlash helped spawn the creation of the so-called Tea Party movement opposing the Democrats' policy program and generating some grassroots energy for Republicans. The Democrats then turned to other legislative priorities, such as a "cap-and-trade" bill as a way to deal with climate change, which passed the House on a slim 219–212 vote, with 44 Democrats voting "no" and just 8 Republicans voting "yes."[70] It died in the Democratic-held Senate, so Speaker Pelosi had forced her members to take a hard vote for a bill that did not become law.

But the most notable policy fight of the 111th Congress came over health care. The Democrats, at what would end up being great political cost, eventually passed the Affordable Care Act, dubbed by Republicans as "Obamacare." The bill would expand health insurance coverage to millions of Americans, but it remained largely unpopular[71] throughout Obama's presidency, and Republicans campaigned against it heavily over the remainder of his time in office. The massive expansion of the social safety net—arguably the biggest new entitlement program since Lyndon Johnson's Great Society programs of the 1960s—put many of the moderate/conservative Democrats in a pickle. Ultimately, 34 Democrats and every Republican voted against the final version of the Obamacare bill.[72]

While the economy did begin to pick up in Obama's first two years, the recovery was slow. The combination of economic angst, opposition to the Democratic policy program, and the overextended Democratic majority would have disastrous electoral consequences.

Republicans smashed the Democratic majority, netting 64 seats and winning a majority bigger than any they had held in the 1990s and 2000s, 242–193. As part of that victory, they defeated 52 incumbents. The usual midterm penalty for the presidential party swung against the Obama White House. And nationalization, which Democrats had bucked to some degree in their victories in 2006 and 2008, reemerged in great force: after winning 49 McCain-won districts in 2008, Democratic House candidates carried only 12 in 2010.

A study by top political scientists found that voting for the Affordable Care Act exerted a major electoral penalty on Democrats who backed the bill.[73] But strategic voting by Democrats who did not back the bill didn't save many of them: fully half of the 34 Democrats who voted "no" lost in November. Some of the Democratic losers were veteran party leaders, such as Reps. Jim Oberstar (D, MN-8), Ike Skelton (D, MO-4), and John Spratt (D, SC-5), although these members occupied either conservative territory (Skelton and Spratt) or territory that would move right over the course of the following decade (Oberstar in Minnesota's Iron Range). Conservative representative Gene Taylor (D, MS-4) was another loser; so was Rep. Stephanie Herseth Sandlin (D, SD-AL), the 2004 special-election winner, and Rep. Chet Edwards (D, TX-17).

Other Republican gains came as a direct rollback of the Democrats' 2006 and 2008 gains: of the 66 Democratic-held seats the Republicans won, 39 had been flipped by Democrats in either 2006 or 2008. As part of this reversal, Republicans essentially restored their original gerrymanders in states like Ohio and Pennsylvania and also netted 5 seats in New York, where they had lost so much ground in the previous couple of cycles. Some of the Republicans who won those seats had lost them in those previous wave years, like Charlie Bass (R, NH-2), Steve Chabot (R, OH-1), and Mike Fitzpatrick (R, PA-8).

There was a strong regional trend to the House results that reflected longer-term partisan shifts. The Republicans made another huge leap in the Greater South, netting 23 seats in the region and grabbing 104 of 145 possible seats, or 72 percent of the districts. In the usually Republican Interior West, Democrats actually had gained a tiny and rare majority, 20–18, in 2008, but Republicans netted 10 seats, restoring regular Republican order to the region, 28–10. The competitive but often GOP-leaning Midwest gave the Republicans a 17-seat net gain.

The Northeast and West Coast proved more resistant to the GOP. While the Republicans did net 13 seats in the Northeast, 10 of those came in just two states: Pennsylvania and New York (where the Democrats had built an unrealistically large edge). Both of New Hampshire's seats flipped, but Democrats held on to all the seats they had gained in 2006 and 2008 in Connecticut and also retained their monopoly in Massachusetts. The Republicans gained only a single seat on the West Coast, as Jamie Herrera Beutler (R, WA-3) won an open seat in southwest Washington State. So even though the GOP enjoyed a massive wave, that wave reinforced some preexisting regional trends.

As part of the 2010 wave, the Republicans also enjoyed smashing successes down the ballot, netting hundreds of state legislative seats and flipping the governorships of several important states, such as Michigan, Ohio, Pennsylvania, and Wisconsin. This would give the Republicans immense power over the new district maps that would be drawn in response to the 2010 census. Redistricting had not been a direct part of their 2010 victories, as no maps changed between 2008 and 2010, although one could argue that they benefited from their old gerrymanders in states like Ohio and Pennsylvania. But now, with the power of the pen in many places, Republicans would seek to lock in or even expand their newly regained advantage in the House.

2012–16: THE GOP RETRENCHES

House elected (2012): 234–201 Republican
Change from previous election: +8 Democratic
House elected (2014): 247–188 Republican
Change from previous election: +13 Republican
House elected (2016): 241–194 Republican
Change from previous election: +6 Democratic

Republicans came into the new redistricting cycle controlling the drawing of 193 seats while Democrats controlled just 44.[74] In many instances, Republicans tried to lock in the big delegations they had just won in several key states. In others, they tried to create new and more significant advantages.

The Democrats' "worst redistricting devastation" came in North Carolina, where Republicans had won control of the state legislature in 2010.[75] Even though North Carolina had a Democratic governor, the governor has no power over redistricting (unlike in many other states). Newly empowered Republicans undid a previous Democratic gerrymander and imposed their own, flipping a seven-to-six Democratic delegation to a nine-to-four Republican one that would have performed even better had moderate representative Mike McIntyre (D, NC-7) not improbably survived.

Many other GOP gerrymanders were designed to protect what they had won in the 2010 wave. For instance, Republicans had won a 13–5 advantage in Ohio in 2010, which was even better than the 12–6 edge they held at the start of the decade. Ohio, which was losing population share relative to other states, lost two seats in the 2012 reapportionment. Republicans eliminated one Republican seat and one Democratic seat but otherwise drew a map intended to elect 12 Republicans and 4 Democrats, which the map successfully did throughout the decade.

Pennsylvania Republicans, who had to eliminate one seat, drew what analyst Sean Trende suggested might be "the gerrymander of the decade." It combined western Pennsylvania representatives Jason Altmire (D) and

Mark Critz (D) into a reconfigured PA-12 in ancestrally Democratic but Republican-trending western Pennsylvania.[76] The map had its desired effect: Critz beat Altmire in the primary and then lost to Keith Rothfus (R) in November; a 13–5 GOP majority in a competitive state appeared locked in.

In Michigan, where a GOP-drawn map produced a 9–6 Republican delegation in four of the five elections in the 2000s (the only exception was 2008, when the Democrats took a fleeting eight-to-seven lead) in a competitive, Democratic-leaning state, Republican line drawers combined two Democrats into one district and seemed to lock in a 9–5 delegation. Wisconsin did not lose any seats, but Republicans there successfully solidified the state's 5–3 GOP delegation. (Republicans had netted two seats there in 2010.)

Barack Obama would go on to carry all four states (Michigan, Ohio, Pennsylvania, and Wisconsin) in November 2012 with an aggregate 52 percent of the vote, but at the same time Democrats only won 30 percent of the House seats in these battleground states (17 of 56).

This heartland story makes it seem as though Democrats lost out through reapportionment, which continued to move seats from the Northeast and Midwest to the faster-growing South and West. But that's actually not what happened. If one traces the partisan fate of the seats shifted through reapportionment, 8 Democratic seats and 4 Republican ones were effectively eliminated. But the Democrats won 8 of the 12 new seats created elsewhere. Part of that involved certain limits on Republican line drawers in fast-growing Florida and Texas.

In Florida, Republicans controlled the process in a competitive, growing state that was adding two seats. The Republicans had won 19 of 25 seats there in 2010 but were at least somewhat constrained by new voter-approved constitutional amendments that aimed to make the line-drawing process less partisan. Republicans ceded the two new seats to the Democrats and otherwise tried to protect their existing seats, but Democrats ended up picking up two other seats thanks to poor GOP candidates: controversial representative Allen West (R, FL-18) narrowly lost in a seat largely new to him, and Rep. David Rivera (R, FL-26) lost after being embroiled in several scandals.[77] Still, Republicans retained a 17–10 advantage in the delegation. Here was another state that was competitive at the statewide level but where Republicans held a clear majority of the House seats.

In Texas, a long series of legal machinations led to both sides getting two of the state's four new seats. Amazingly, in a state with 36 House districts, only a single one really seemed competitive at the start of the decade: TX-23, which stretched from El Paso to San Antonio.[78] After Ciro Rodriguez (D) lost the seat to Quico Canseco (R) in 2010, Pete Gallego (D) won it back in 2012. The Texas delegation was 24–12 Republican, though.

Some states with nonpartisan redistricting systems produced results that didn't seem to reflect the core partisanship of their states, at least from the standpoint of the 2012 election. Arizona, a state Democrats had won only twice in the postwar era, created a map that allowed Democrats a 5–4 House edge in 2012. Meanwhile, in New Jersey, the delegation split 6–6 even though the Garden State had become comfortably Democratic at the presidential level.

California, site of a static incumbent protection plan in the 2000s, instituted nonpartisan redistricting through a citizens' commission method via ballot initiative in 2010. This formally robbed Democrats of gerrymandering power, even though they had won the governorship along with big state legislative majorities in 2010. But the map they got through the nonpartisan system would, in all likelihood, become better for them than anything they could've created themselves. This was not necessarily an accident, ProPublica reported: "The citizens' commission had pledged to create districts based on testimony from the communities themselves, not from parties or statewide political players. To get around that, Democrats surreptitiously enlisted local voters, elected officials, labor unions and community groups to testify in support of configurations that coincided with the party's interests."[79] However, California was also changing and becoming more Democratic, a trend that would generally continue throughout the decade.

As it was, Democrats netted four seats in the state, and it really should have been five. California voters also created a new "top-two" election system via 2010 ballot issue, which meant that instead of holding traditional primaries, all candidates would run together on the same ballot, and the top two finishers, regardless of party, would advance to the November election. This frustrated Democrats in the newly drawn and Democratic-leaning CA-31 in San Bernardino County; a split in the Democratic vote allowed two Republicans to advance to the general election.

Democrats were not entirely without redistricting power. In Illinois, they eliminated one Republican seat to deal with reapportionment and then beat four Republican incumbents on Election Day, flipping an 11–8 GOP delegation into a 12–6 Democratic one. In Maryland, a Democratic gerrymander effectively made it impossible for Rep. Roscoe Bartlett (R, MD-6) to win, and John Delaney (D) beat him, creating a 7–1 Democratic delegation in the increasingly Democratic state.

Not everything in 2012 was about redistricting. Democrats fought back to recapture both seats in New Hampshire, restoring a uniformly Democratic delegation in New England. Meanwhile, Republicans captured some seats that voted heavily for losing GOP presidential candidate Mitt Romney, like the open seats AR-4, IN-2, and OK-2, as well as KY-6, where narrow 2010 survivor Rep. Ben Chandler (D), the 2004 special-election winner, fell to Andy Barr (R).

Obama's reduced national margin of victory (from seven to four points), combined with the nationalization of results and the largely Republican-dominated redistricting, led to a major, historic reduction in the number of crossover districts. Only 26 districts featured split results for House and president: Republicans won 17 Obama-won districts, and Democrats won just 9 Romney-won districts. So only 6 percent of districts featured crossover results; that was the lowest percentage in any presidential election year since at least 1920.[80] Overall, Democrats netted eight seats, cutting the GOP majority to 234–201. This was still a bigger GOP majority than any that Republicans had won during their previous dozen years of power from 1995 to 2007.

To get a sense as to the GOP advantage on the overall House map, consider that even though Obama won the national popular vote by four points, 51–47, Romney carried a clear majority of districts, 229, while Obama carried just 206. Similarly, Democrats won the national House popular vote by about a point and half, but that translated into only about

46 percent of all the seats. Part of the problem for Democrats is that they were wasting votes in more places than Republicans: for instance, Obama won two-thirds or more of the vote in 81 districts while Romney won two-thirds of the vote in just 33. This provided some backing for political scientist Jonathan Rodden's argument that the Democratic vote is inefficiently distributed nationally. At the same time, it's also clear from a state-by-state analysis that the Republicans used their redistricting power to great effect in many key states in 2012.

The Democrats retaining control of the White House suggested that Republicans would easily hold the House in 2014, given the usual midterm presidential penalty and Obama's mediocre approval rating. That is indeed what happened. Republicans only netted 13 seats, but that gain gave them a 247–188 majority, their biggest since just before the Great Depression. The results, in general, featured a further sorting along partisan lines. They also provided a preview of the tumultuous 2016 presidential election in some instances.

It was an ominous sign for Democrats that two of their few remaining members on Republican turf, Reps. Jim Matheson (D, UT-4) and Mike McIntyre (D, NC-7), decided to retire. Both were narrow winners in 2012, and it would prove impossible for Democrats to hold their seats; the GOP takeover made real the intended result of the North Carolina Republicans' House gerrymander: a 10–3 GOP delegation that took two cycles instead of just one to realize. Republicans also beat Reps. John Barrow (D, GA-12) and Nick Rahall (D, WV-3) by healthy margins in strong Romney districts. Barrow had been the last White male Democratic House member from the Deep South, and Rahall's loss meant that Republicans now held all three House seats in West Virginia. The state's shift toward favoring Republicans at the presidential level, first evident in 2000, had now bled down the ballot.

Democrats did successfully navigate the California top-two primary in CA-31 to score a rare pickup. Democrats also beat Reps. Steve Southerland (R, FL-2) and Lee Terry (R, NE-2) in competitive Romney-won seats after both incumbents alienated constituents with a series of boneheaded moves and statements: Southerland, running against Gwen Graham (daughter of a popular former senator and governor), held a "men-only" fundraiser, while Terry seemed out of touch when he argued that House members should be paid during a government shutdown in October 2013.[81] These three seats represented the extent of Democratic gains; the party was powerless against all other Republicans, including even Rep. Michael Grimm (R, NY-11), who, despite running under indictment on federal fraud charges, easily won reelection (he would resign before the opening of the new Congress).

Republicans would net five seats by rolling back Democratic gains from two years prior, and they would also score victories in Obama-won districts such as IA-1, IL-12, and ME-2, all districts that were largely White and had below-average levels of four-year college degree attainment. It was not clear at the time, but these were the kinds of places that would shift very heavily toward Republican presidential nominee Donald Trump two years later. All told, the number of crossover districts grew from 26 to 31. But there were only 5 Democrats left in Romney-won seats and 26 Republicans in Obama-won seats.

The most notable results of the election came in the primary season: House majority leader Eric Cantor (R, VA-7) lost to Dave Brat (R) in a shocking result. Cantor was arguably in line to be Speaker of the House, as Speaker John Boehner (R, OH-8) ended up announcing his resignation in late 2015. While Cantor was one of just four House members to lose primaries in 2014, his defeat contributed to a growing feeling that the Republican base was in a state of revolt against the party's leadership.

But that was nothing compared to the nomination of Donald Trump to lead the party's presidential ticket in 2016. Trump's Republican primary victory, and early polling showing him generally performing weakly compared to other Republican possibilities against eventual Democratic nominee Hillary Clinton, seemed to open up the possibility that a wave against Trump could win Democrats not just the presidency for a third straight time but also the House.

Assisting the Democratic cause were new congressional maps in Florida and Virginia. The Florida Supreme Court imposed a new map in advance of the 2016 elections after finding that Republicans had violated the "fair districts" standards that Florida voters enshrined in the state constitution in 2010. The changes were not extreme, but the alterations contributed to the Democrats winning three GOP-held seats, FL-7, FL-10, and FL-13. However, the district lines also changed in FL-2, where Graham had scored her upset in 2014. Her district became unwinnable for a Democrat, so she opted not to run again. All told, Democrats netted two seats as a result of the Florida remap. In the Old Dominion, a federal court found that Republican line drawers had packed too many Black voters in Rep. Bobby Scott's (D, VA-3) heavily Democratic district. In unwinding portions of that district, the court made the seat of Rep. Randy Forbes (R, VA-4) into a Democratic seat. He ran in a primary for an open neighboring seat, but he lost; meanwhile, Don McEachin (D) won the new VA-4. That netted the Democrats another new seat they otherwise would not have won. (North Carolina also had to draw a new map in response to a racial gerrymandering finding, but Republicans were able to do so in such a way as to preserve their 10–3 edge in the delegation.)

Unfortunately for Democrats, they did not win much new beyond their redistricting gains. They only netted six seats nationally in the midst of an election in which presidential results at the district level diverged quite dramatically from those of 2012. Even though Clinton won the popular vote by two points, just two points worse than Obama four years earlier, nearly half the seats, 200 of 435, saw at least a five-percentage-point change in Democratic or Republican presidential performance (or both).[82] Journalists Ron Brownstein and Leah Askarinam found that "from the presidency through lower-ballot races, Republicans rely on a preponderantly white coalition that is strongest among whites without a college degree and those living outside of major metropolitan areas. Democrats depend on a heavily urbanized (and often postindustrial) upstairs-downstairs coalition of minorities, many of them clustered in lower-income inner-city districts. They also rely on more affluent college-educated whites both in cities and inner suburbs." Specifically, they found that Democrats won 87 of 108 districts that had higher-than-average percentages of White college graduates and racial minorities, while Republicans controlled 152 of 176 districts that had lower-than-average percentages of White college graduates and minorities.[83]

A few races featured rematches, most notably in the upscale, highly educated Chicago suburban district IL-10, where ex-representative Brad

Schneider (D) beat Rep. Robert Dold (R) in the rubber match of their three-cycle battle (Schneider beat Dold in 2012, and then Dold beat Schneider in 2014). Dold could not overcome Trump's roughly 30-point deficit in the district. In NH-1, a classic swing seat that Trump barely carried, ex-representative Carol Shea-Porter (D) narrowly beat scandal-tinged representative Frank Guinta (R) as they battled in a general election for the fourth straight time (the Republican won in 2010 and 2014, the Democrat in 2012 and 2016). Shea-Porter would retire in 2018, and Guinta decided not to run again. Democrats held the seat. Republicans won back NE-2, lost in 2014 thanks to a weak candidate, and the open FL-18, which they had lost in 2012 (and had been untouched by redistricting). Both seats had been won by Trump, although not overwhelmingly.

Rep. Scott Garrett (R, NJ-5), who had pushed out the more moderate Marge Roukema (R) almost a decade and a half earlier in a northern New Jersey district, fell to business-friendly Josh Gottheimer (D), who ran against Garrett's extremism: the incumbent had refused to donate to the National Republican Congressional Committee over its backing of gay candidates.[84] That Trump ran below usual GOP performance in the district (he won by one after Romney had won by three) couldn't have helped Garrett.

All told, the House elections of 2012, 2014, and 2016 were defined by stability. Over the course of the three elections, Democrats made an aggregate gain of just a single seat (they netted 14, combined, in 2012 and 2016, but lost 13 in 2014). Trump couldn't deliver Democrats the House in 2016—not even close. But his presence in the White House opened the door to the possibility of a Democratic takeover in 2018.

2018: THE BLUE WAVE RESTORES THE DEMOCRATIC MAJORITY

House elected (2018): 235–200 Democratic
Change from previous election: +41 Democratic

Republicans found themselves back in total control of Washington in 2017. It may have been that this was not the outcome many voters in 2016 expected.

Instead of prompting a backlash, perceptions of Trump as a general-election underdog may have actually aided Republican House efforts. Writing in advance of the 2016 presidential election, political scientist Robert Erikson found that in post–World War II presidential elections, a small but important group of well-informed voters may vote against the party of the candidate they perceive will win the White House as a way of providing a check on the president in the presidential year, as opposed to waiting for the midterm two years later to provide that balance. Betting markets, pundits, and the general public all saw Clinton as the favorite in the presidential election.[85] Following the election, Erikson speculated that these perceptions may have hurt Democratic House performance: "Plausibly, many who thought Hillary Clinton would win voted Republican for Congress to block, thus accounting for the Democrats' surprisingly feeble performance at the congressional level in 2016."[86] While the differences were subtle, Trump lost the popular presidential vote by two points while House Republicans won the overall House vote by about a point. But in several Clinton-won, affluent, highly educated House districts—the kinds of places one might expect to find some of those sophisticated voters Erikson identified as potential presidential-year ticket splitters—Republican House incumbents such as Reps. Mike Coffman (R, CO-6) in suburban Denver, Barbara Comstock (R, VA-10) in northern Virginia, and Erik Paulsen (R, MN-3) in Minnesota's Twin Cities suburbs all ran at least 15 percentage points ahead of Trump in terms of margin in their districts.

Had Clinton actually won the White House, they all may have been fine in 2018. Clinton's approval, just like Trump's, could have been bad, and the usual out-party midterm trend would have been working against the Democrats, not the Republicans. But Trump's win put many of these seemingly strong incumbents in much more serious danger than their impressive 2016 victories would have otherwise suggested. Democrats, enraged by Trump's victory, activated strongly, the way a party locked out of power often does during a midterm election. One sign of Democratic engagement was historic fundraising by Democratic House challengers to Republican incumbents: Democratic candidates "shattered all previous records for challenger fundraising," wrote campaign finance expert Michael Malbin. The previous high-water mark had been set by Republican challengers in 2010, and their fundraising contributed to the GOP's strong performance that year. As noted in chapter 2, challenger fundraising is often a more important electoral indicator than incumbent fundraising.[87]

A closely watched special election in metro Atlanta would provide something of a preview of what was to come in 2018. Trump elevated Rep. Tom Price (R, GA-6) to be secretary of Health and Human Services, opening up his district—which, at one time and under different lines, had been held by Newt Gingrich—and forcing a special election. Romney had carried the district by 23 points in 2012, but Trump only won the highly educated suburban seat by 1.5 points. Still, even as that presidential shift was occurring, Price had won easily in 2016. Republicans would hold the district in a June 2017 special-election runoff but only by about 3.5 points, indicating that this was no longer a safe Republican seat. While Democrats were disappointed in the result of what became the most expensive House race of all time—the *Atlantic*'s Molly Ball called it a "gut punch to Democrats' confidence"[88]—it was an early indication that some of the shifts against Trump in usually Republican suburban districts were negatively affecting non-Trump Republican candidates.

Republican governance also imperiled the GOP majority. Health care, which had helped destroy Democratic majorities in 1994 and 2010, contributed to the Republican demise in 2018. During Barack Obama's presidency, Republicans railed against Obamacare, which was the signature achievement stemming from Obama and the Democrats' brief unified control of Washington from 2009 to 2010. Republicans, and Trump, vowed to "repeal and replace" Obamacare. However, when given the opportunity, Republicans failed to pass an alternative. The GOP spent much of the first half of 2017 trying to get a repeal through the House, initially failing but then succeeding. That bill narrowly died in the GOP-controlled Senate, however, meaning that several vulnerable Republicans found themselves compelled to cast a difficult vote on a bill that didn't even become law. It was reminiscent of the "cap-and-trade" climate change bill that was a tough vote for many moderate Democrats in 2009. That bill never even got a vote in the Democratic-controlled Senate after passing the House. Meanwhile, public sentiment about Obamacare became more positive throughout 2017 and 2018, and the RealClearPolitics national polling average showed net favorability for

Obamacare improving from being net negative before Trump took office to net positive after.[89]

That a liberal policy became more popular after a conservative government took over is very much in keeping with the rhythms of public opinion. Public opinion expert James Stimson notes how the public's policy preferences can oscillate between the two parties depending on which one of them is in power: "Preferences 'zig' upward (toward liberalism) when Republicans control the White House and 'zag' downward when Democrats are in charge."[90] Not only did Republicans not achieve the policy objective they desired—doing away with Obamacare—they also found themselves open to Democratic attacks on the health-care issue as Democratic candidates emphasized issues like maintaining Obamacare's popular insurance protections for people with preexisting medical conditions.

Democrats also benefited from redistricting in Pennsylvania, where the state's Democratic-majority supreme court interpreted state law to force the unwinding of the Republican-drawn gerrymander. The court replaced it with a map that was not necessarily a Democratic gerrymander but "consistently makes subtle choices that nudge districts in the direction of Democrats," according to political analyst Nate Cohn.[91] The map altered the whole state, turning a map that Republicans drew to elect 13 Republicans and 5 Democrats to the House into one in which Democrats seemed guaranteed to make significant gains. It radically reconfigured a southeast Pennsylvania seat held by Rep. Pat Meehan (R), turning it from a heavily gerrymandered swing seat into a district that Clinton would have won by about 30 points in 2016. Meehan had already announced his retirement partly because of a sexual harassment scandal, but no Republican could realistically hold this seat under the new lines. Rep. Charlie Dent (R), who represented a Republican-leaning seat that included most of the Lehigh Valley, had also already decided to retire. His seat went from one that Trump won by eight points to a more compact district that Clinton won by a point. Another southeast Pennsylvania seat, held by Rep. Ryan Costello (R), also became significantly more Democratic, prompting Costello to retire. In western Pennsylvania, Rep. Conor Lamb (D)—who had already won a March 2018 special election in a strongly Republican district under the old map—got a much less Republican, albeit

Trump-won, district to run in and easily defeated Rep. Keith Rothfus (R) in a member-versus-member contest in the Pittsburgh suburbs.

All told, Democrats went from holding five seats in Pennsylvania at the start of the cycle to forcing a 9–9 tie with Republicans. What's interesting to consider, though, is the possibility that Democrats could have netted four seats on the old gerrymandered Republican map too. It's clear that Lamb was capable of winning his district under the old map, because he won it in a March special election under the old lines. Additionally, because Dent and Meehan both eventually resigned, special elections were held in November for their old seats to fill their unexpired terms along with regular elections for the new districts. Democrats ended up winning the districts under the old lines as well as the new, although by much-reduced margins in the old districts. Had his district not been altered, Costello may very well have run for reelection and could have held his seat (but, then again, perhaps not).

Ultimately, the net change in Pennsylvania may have been the same without the new map, but the Democratic victories there under less favorable lines probably would have required significantly more effort and investment from Democrats. As it was, all four of the Democratic pickups in Pennsylvania came by double-digit margins.

Following the Pennsylvania redistricting, Republicans controlled 25 districts that Hillary Clinton had won in 2016, and Democrats controlled 13 districts that Donald Trump had carried. These were naturally the most vulnerable seats on both sides. Republicans ended up picking up just three previously Democratic seats in 2018 and, perhaps unsurprisingly, all three of them were open seats in Republican-leaning turf. One of those was Pennsylvania's redesigned PA-14, which was an even more Republican-leaning version of the district Lamb won in the special election and then left behind; the other two, MN-1 and MN-8, both voted for Trump by about 15 points in 2016 after voting for Obama four years earlier, and they were two of the relatively few remaining largely White and rural districts that Democrats held anywhere in the country.

Meanwhile, Democrats ended up winning all *but* three of the Clinton-Republican districts. Many of the Democratic victories came in well-to-do suburban areas with higher-than-average rates of four-year college attainment. Coffman, Comstock, and Paulsen—three of the Republicans mentioned earlier that ran well ahead of Trump in 2016—all lost in relative blowout fashion, falling by double digits to well-heeled Democratic challengers. The suburban voters who shifted to Clinton in 2016—but not to Democratic House candidates—could not vote against Trump in 2018, so they did what for them was the next best way to register their disapproval: vote against their congressional Republican representatives.

To show how much had changed over the course of the decade, the Democratic gerrymander of Illinois designed the districts of both Reps. Peter Roskam (R, IL-6) and Randy Hultgren (R, IL-14) to be safe Republican seats in the Chicagoland suburbs/exurbs. By 2018, Democrats had beaten both incumbents.[92] One could argue that the Illinois remap ended up being a Democratic dummymander, as Democrats designed it to position themselves to win a couple of downstate districts that they either never won during the decade (IL-13) or won only once in 2012 and then lost the rest of the decade (IL-12). But unanticipated political changes throughout the decade, particularly in those suburban districts that Democrats won in 2018, meant that Democrats captured a 13–5 edge in the Land of Lincoln, better than the 12–6 edge they won in 2012, the first election contested under the Democratic gerrymander. Democrats also pulled to a 7–7 tie in the Michigan delegation despite that state's Republican gerrymander. There they won neighboring seats (MI-8 and MI-11) running west of Detroit that covered some of the city's suburbs and exurbs as well as the state capital of Lansing. But Republican gerrymanders in Wisconsin and Ohio held firm, even though Democrats came close to winning an August special election in OH-12, which covered suburban, exurban, and rural turf north and east of Columbus.

The Democratic near-sweep in Clinton districts stood out, but in addition to winning 22 of those 25 districts, the Democrats made similar gains among the Trump-won districts, picking off 21 in total. About half of them, 10, were only marginal Trump districts—ones he won by less than five points. One of those was a district made famous in the earlier special election: GA-6, in the Atlanta suburbs, where Lucy McBath (D), a Black candidate who ran for office after losing a son to gun violence, succeeded in beating Rep. Karen Handel (R), the special-election winner.

McBath, like many other Democratic candidates, emphasized gun control as part of her platform; unlike 2006, when Democrats won the House in part because of culturally conservative candidates running in right-of-center districts, it was hard to classify many (if any) of this new crop of Democrats as being consistently conservative on hot-button social issues such as gun control, abortion, and same-sex marriage. That said, there were some Democrats elected in 2018 who did run as pro-gun candidates: examples include Lamb in western Pennsylvania, Jeff Van Drew (D, NJ-2), and Jared Golden (D, ME-2). Golden merits mention as an unusual winner: he finished narrowly behind Rep. Bruce Poliquin (R), but because Poliquin did not receive a majority of the vote, the state's new ranked-choice voting system kicked in and allowed Golden to win because he had gotten more second-place votes. The Democrats once again held every seat in the six states of New England. Van Drew also ended up being an unusual member of the House for reasons that will become clear in the 2020 section.

Democrats also won a handful of districts that went to Trump by double-digit margins. Perhaps the two biggest surprises came in Charleston and Oklahoma City, where Joe Cunningham (D, SC-1) and Kendra Horn (D, OK-5) won in upsets. Still, even these victories fit within the overall trend, as both districts cover urban/suburban turf, and Trump ran behind Romney's 2012 margin in both.

All told, Democrats ended up winning a 235–200 majority in a 2018 election cycle that did not really end until September of the following year because of a do-over election in North Carolina. Rep. Robert Pittenger (R, NC-9) lost a primary to Mark Harris, a former pastor who had nearly beaten Pittenger in a 2016 primary. Harris faced veteran Dan McCready (D) in the general election in a GOP-leaning district that covers part of the Charlotte suburbs while sprawling east along the South Carolina border. On election night, it appeared that Harris had won by almost 900 votes, but there was a catch: the state refused to certify the results because of emerging (and credible) accusations of fraud involving absentee ballots. That led to a new election. Harris declined to run again, and state senator Dan Bishop (R) took his place as the GOP nominee against McCready. Bishop won by two points in the election rerun held in September 2019, closing the books on the 2018 election. Here again, a GOP gerrymander held.

If redistricting and realignment helped build the GOP's House majority, it can also be said that those factors helped destroy it, at least in 2018. Trump's candidacy accelerated a preexisting trend in which White voters without a four-year college degree were becoming more Republican, while White voters with a four-year college degree were becoming more Democratic. These trends manifested themselves in the House results, contributing to immense vulnerability for Republicans in previously safe affluent suburban districts across the country. Democrats got a slight boost from new districts that replaced GOP gerrymanders in some places, although this was not the decisive factor in their ability to win a majority (although without new maps in Florida, Pennsylvania, and Virginia, the Democratic majority would have been smaller).

So beyond redistricting and realignment, there was another *r*—reaction, as in the negative reaction to the election and actions of President Donald Trump—that played a role. Holding the White House would once again be a curse for the president's party in the House.

2020: BLUE RIPPLE, BIG SORT

House elected (2020): 222–213 Democratic
Change from previous election: +13 Republican

Following the 2018 election, the Democrats held 31 districts carried by Donald Trump in the 2016 election, while Republicans held only 3 Hillary Clinton–won districts. All three of those Clinton-seat Republicans held marginal seats where she did not exceed 50 percent of the vote.

Democrats were also pushing the limits of what was plausible even in Democratic-dominated California, where the party had picked up seven new seats in 2018, creating a lopsided 46–7 advantage in that state. While the Democrats did this without having to win a single district carried by Trump—an indicator of just how Democratic California had become—they captured several seats in Southern California that had flipped from voting for Romney in 2012 to Clinton in 2016 but were otherwise historically Republican (such as several covering Orange County, one of the nerve centers of Goldwater/Reagan-style conservatism). The 2020 election would test how Democratic they had truly become beyond the presidential ballot.

So the Democrats were overextended in the House heading into the 2020 presidential contest, in which Donald Trump would seek a second term against Barack Obama's vice president, Joe Biden. But Democrats nonetheless appeared well positioned to hold and even expand their majority throughout the election cycle.

Part of the reason for that belief among analysts was another midde-cade redistricting that at least partially undid a Republican gerrymander. State courts in North Carolina, led by a Democratic-controlled state supreme court, ordered the state's legislative and congressional districts redrawn because they were gerrymandered. This would lead to the decade's third congressional map in North Carolina—remember that state Republicans had redrawn the map once before, in advance of the 2016 election, to address a racial gerrymandering ruling. Republicans were able to preserve a 10–3 edge in the delegation on the new map, but after the state court ruling, Republicans grudgingly drew a new map that effectively gave the Democrats two new seats, one in the Raleigh area and one representing Greensboro/Winston-Salem. Hillary Clinton carried both of the newly drawn seats by roughly 20 points in 2016, and Democrats easily won both in the 2020 election as the Republican incumbents who held the prior versions of those seats, Reps. George Holding (R, NC-2) and Mark Walker (R, NC-6), retired.[93]

Retirements, more broadly, also seemed to benefit Democrats. Of the 41 Democratic seats rated as competitive in the final *Sabato's Crystal Ball* House ratings, 40 were being defended by incumbents. Meanwhile, of the 48 Republican-held seats listed, 14 did not have incumbents running for reelection in the general election.[94] The list of vulnerable Republican-held open seats was led by one of the three Clinton-won districts Republicans defended in 2018: Rep. Will Hurd (R) of the frequently competitive and geographically huge San Antonio–to–El Paso TX-23, retired, giving Democrats a prime target in a majority-Hispanic district they had narrowly lost in 2018. Republican incumbents also retired in a number of traditionally Republican suburban districts with higher-than-average levels of four-year college degree attainment, such as GA-7 in greater Atlanta, IN-5 in the Indianapolis suburbs, TX-22 in the Houston area, and TX-24 in the Dallas–Ft. Worth metroplex. Trump had carried all of these districts in 2016, but by reduced margins from what Republicans usually got. In other words, these districts represented the potential for Democrats to cut even deeper into the suburbs. On the Democratic side, the only truly vulnerable open seat was IA-2, an Obama-to-Trump White working-class district in southeast Iowa. Democratic House incumbents in the most vulnerable districts generally were still raising gobs of money, but many of their Republican challengers were doing well too, as Michael Malbin, the campaign finance expert, noted along with his colleague Brendan Glavin in late February 2020.[95]

The primary season also seemed to open up potential new Republican vulnerabilities. In western Colorado (CO-3) and central Virginia (VA-5), hard-right candidates won the nominations over Republican incumbent representatives Scott Tipton and Denver Riggleman, respectively, in districts Trump had carried by about a dozen points apiece, adding new defensive responsibilities for Republicans. However, Republicans arguably benefited from some of their other primary losers: Reps. Ross Spano (R, FL-15), Steve King (R, IA-4), and Steve Watkins (R, KS-2) all had various liabilities but were replaced by less problematic nominees who all held these seats in the fall. Three Democratic primary losers, Reps. Dan Lipinski (D, IL-3), Lacy Clay (D, MO-1), and Eliot Engel (D, NY-16), lost to more liberal challengers in safe Democratic seats (Lipinski was one of the least liberal members of the Democratic caucus and one of the few who did not support abortion rights).

The presidential election loomed large over the House elections—to a degree unseen in a century or more. Early in 2020, it seemed as though Trump could win another term—he was not a favorite, but he was not a huge underdog either. Perceptions of his handling of the economy were better[96] than his overall weak approval rating, and he survived an impeachment fight: on almost entirely party-line votes, the House voted to impeach and the Senate to acquit Trump of charges of abuse of power and obstruction of Congress related to a seeming attempt to obtain from the Ukrainian government what amounted to opposition research on Biden, who at the time was not yet the Democratic presidential nominee.

The impeachment fight ended up costing the Democrats a member: Rep. Jeff Van Drew (D, NJ-2), one of the party's Trump district members who had just been elected in 2018, switched parties over impeachment. He may have lost a Democratic primary had he not crossed over. Democrats lost an additional seat when they couldn't defend a vacancy in CA-25, a Romney-to-Clinton Southern California seat flipped by Rep. Katie Hill (D) in 2018. Hill resigned in late 2019 after explicit photos of her were leaked online and as she faced allegations of inappropriate relationships with staffers. Veteran Mike Garcia (R) won the seat by an impressive 10 points in a May special election, although analysts believed he would face a tougher race in the fall with presidential-level turnout.[97]

The national focus shifted, though, as a once-in-a-century pandemic, COVID-19, introduced a new overarching issue to the election. By Election Day, the disease had contributed to roughly a quarter of a million deaths, and the public generally gave the president poor marks for his handling of the pandemic.

Throughout the summer and fall, the political environment seemed as though it would be similar enough to 2018 to sustain the Democrats' new House majority and then some. According to FiveThirtyEight's weighted average, Democrats led in the House generic ballot polling by a little over seven points, not that much different from the 8.5-point lead the party enjoyed before the 2018 election. Biden led Trump by about 8.5 points in FiveThirtyEight's national polling average as well.

But for the second straight presidential election cycle, polls underestimated Trump, who still lost to Biden, but only by about 4.5 points nationally. And were it not for a combined roughly 43,000-vote Biden plurality in Arizona, Georgia, and Wisconsin, Biden's 306–232 Electoral College win over Trump would've been a 269–269 tie. That tie would have been resolved in the House of Representatives, where Trump likely would have won because of the way ties are broken (all 50 states get a single vote, and Republicans controlled a majority of the House delegations despite not winning a majority of seats).[98]

While Biden's popular-vote victory ended up being the second largest since 2000, with only Barack Obama's 2008 victory being more decisive, Democrats often lagged Biden in House races, and the combined

Democratic versus Republican House vote in all races only gave the Democrats a roughly three-point edge—or a point and a half smaller than Biden's national edge. Instead of the Democrats padding their majority, Republicans netted 13 seats, cutting the Democrats to just a 222–213 edge after the dust cleared from a vote-counting process extended by the greater prevalence of mail-in voting prompted by concerns over the pandemic.

Overall, the results seemed to reinforce some preexisting trends. The number of crossover districts—those that backed one party for president and the other for House—numbered just 17, the lowest in the post–World War II era (markedly smaller than even the 26 in 2012, the previous postwar record). While records from the early 20th century are incomplete, the percentage of crossover districts probably was at its lowest level since the late 1800s or early 1900s, another era defined by strong party loyalty and limited ticket splitting. Gary Jacobson, the House scholar cited above, found that there was a .987 correlation (with zero being the lowest and one being the highest) between the district-level presidential and House results in 2020, the highest of any presidential election since at least 1952. This was a bit higher than 2012 and 2016, when the correlation was a still very high .950.[99]

Figure 3.3 shows the massive reduction in the number of House districts with split outcomes—one party winning for president and the other winning for House—from 1964 through 2020.

Figure 3.3. Crossover House districts, 1964–2020

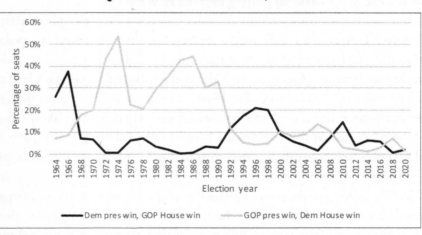

Source: Data compiled and provided by Jonathan Rodden

After Democrats elected 31 members from Trump-won districts in 2018, they elected only seven in 2020. A combination of factors led to this sharp decline.

First of all, Van Drew's party switch reduced the group's ranks by one even before the election, and Van Drew won a competitive reelection as Trump once again carried his South Jersey district. In the actual election, almost half (14) of the 30 remaining Trump-won districts held by Democrats flipped to Biden. The Democrats who held these districts all won reelection, although several had close calls, such as Reps. Lauren Underwood (D, IL-14), Conor Lamb (D, PA-17), and Abigail Spanberger (D, VA-7).

Of the remaining 16, Republicans defeated 8 incumbents. That included long-serving representative Collin Peterson (D, MN-7), the Agriculture Committee chairman who could not survive another 30-point Trump victory in his rural western Minnesota district, especially as Republicans rallied to a challenger, former Lt. Gov. Michelle Fischbach (R), who was more credible and better funded than many of Peterson's past opponents. Overall, Minnesota was illustrative of the partisan sorting of House results. In 2016, four of its eight districts had voted for different parties for House and for president. In 2020, all eight districts voted the same way: Republicans picked up three outstate districts that voted twice for Trump over the course of 2018 and 2020, while Democrats in 2018 flipped two more suburban-focused seats that voted against Trump either once (MN-2, in 2020) or twice (MN-3) and then held these districts in 2020.

Republicans also knocked off Reps. Abby Finkenauer (D, IA-1), Xochitl Torres Small (D, NM-2), Anthony Brindisi (D, NY-22), Max Rose (D, NY-11), Kendra Horn (D, OK-5), Joe Cunningham (D, SC-1), and Ben McAdams (D, UT-4), all first-time 2018 winners who couldn't generate enough crossover support to win again as Trump carried their districts once more. Republicans also flipped the one vulnerable open Democratic seat, the Trump-won IA-2, though only by an incredibly tiny six-vote margin. A few more-seasoned Trump-district members, like Reps. Cheri Bustos (D, IL-17), Matt Cartwright (D, PA-8), and Ron Kind (D, WI-3), held on, but by narrower margins than what they were used to. Bustos served as chairwoman of the Democratic Congressional Campaign Committee, but she only won by four points.

So, to a significant extent, the Democratic Trump 2016 seats sorted themselves out—the lion's share either flipped to Biden and retained their Democratic House incumbents or stuck with Trump and elected Republican House members. Of the remaining Trump-district Democrats, several backed Trump by only a point or less, as was the case in districts retained by first-term representatives Cindy Axne (D, IA-3), Elissa Slotkin (D, MI-8), and Andy Kim (D, NJ-3). Rep. Jared Golden (D, ME-2) won relatively easily even as Trump once again carried the single electoral vote in Maine's Second District for the second straight time. Maine and Nebraska are the only two states that award some of their electoral votes by congressional district as opposed to the other states, which are winner takes all at the statewide level.

The list of Republican victors in Biden-won congressional districts also includes a split electoral vote/House outcome, as Rep. Don Bacon (R, NE-2) won even as Biden carried the electoral vote in his Omaha-based district. Additionally, the only two Republican incumbents running for reelection in 2020 who held 2016 Clinton seats also both won easily, Reps. John Katko (R, NY-24) and Brian Fitzpatrick (R, PA-1).

Republicans also held all but one of their vulnerable open seats—setting aside the two redistricting casualties in North Carolina—losing just GA-7 in the Atlanta suburbs, a rapidly diversifying and highly educated district that flipped from Trump 2016 to Biden 2020. Democrats struck out everywhere else, including the open TX-24, which Biden carried but Republicans held in a close House contest. Democrats had hopes that their candidates could win several seats in Texas and across the suburban industrial North on the strength of Biden's performance, but while Biden improved on Clinton in many of these districts (IN-5, OH-1, PA-10, TX-21, and TX-22), he did not carry any of them, and Republican House incumbents/candidates ran ahead of Trump in all of these districts anyway. Just like in 2016, Republicans in suburban districts may have benefited from ticket splitters who didn't like Trump but had not become Democrats down the ballot and/or anticipated a Biden victory but did not want to fully empower Democrats in Congress.

Republicans enjoyed a rebound in some California districts, narrowly holding CA-25, the seat won by Mike Garcia (R) in the lower-turnout special election and clawing back three of the other seats they had lost in 2018, CA-21 (in the Central Valley), as well as CA-39 and CA-48 in Orange County. Biden still won these diverse districts, but Republican candidates won each at the House level by tiny margins.

Democrats still won a 42–11 edge in the California House delegation, eight seats better than the 34–19 advantage the party held at the start of the decade.

Contributing to the Republican resurgence in California and elsewhere was that Trump ran better with Hispanic voters across the country than he had four years earlier, which aided Republicans in some of the California seats, which are diverse (Trump also likely did better with Asian American voters, and two of the California winners, Young Kim in CA-39 and Michelle Steel in CA-48, are Korean American).[100] Preelection polling picked up on Trump's better numbers with Hispanics, but the size of his improvement didn't become clear until election night when diverse, heavily Hispanic Miami-Dade County reported its results: Clinton's 29-point victory there fell to just 7 for Biden, a shocking drop. This turnabout contributed to Republicans retaking two South Florida districts they had lost in 2018, FL-26 and FL-27, as Trump ran roughly 20 points better in both than he had four years earlier. One of the Democratic losers was Rep. Donna Shalala (D, FL-27), a former secretary of Health and Human Services in the Clinton administration who later served as president of the University of Miami. Shalala, though, was old for a first-time House member (77 when elected in 2018), and she had other liabilities (she did not speak Spanish in a heavily Hispanic district, for instance). She lost reelection even as Biden retained her district, albeit by a significantly reduced margin (Clinton won it by 20 points while Biden won it by only 3).

Another major sign of Democratic weakness among Hispanics came in South Texas, where some small, heavily Hispanic counties swung as far as 50 points in the direction of Trump. TX-23, the open Clinton-won swing seat that seemed like a slam-dunk pickup for Democrats, both flipped to Trump and stuck with Republicans at the House level. In the end, no seats in Texas changed hands, a major disappointment for Democrats, who had hoped to flip several seats there.

In the weeks that followed the election, and as results became finalized, other signs of Democratic erosion among Hispanics emerged across the nation, from places ranging from Massachusetts to Arizona, as compiled by CNN analyst Harry Enten. Why Trump did better with Hispanics was an open question in the aftermath of the election, although, as Enten noted, Trump may have just benefited from incumbency—he was the first Republican incumbent president on the ballot since George W. Bush in 2004, who also turned in a relatively strong performance with Hispanic voters for a Republican presidential candidate.[101] *New York Times* columnist Jamelle Bouie also pointed to the possibility that a round of stimulus checks sent to many Americans to help the economy in the midst of pandemic-related shutdowns helped Trump do better than expected. While Bouie noted that political shifts can have many explanations, to some extent the Republicans' "strong performance can be explained simply by the fact that it was the party in power when the government put a lot of money into the hands of a lot of people who didn't have it before."[102] The Democratic research firm Equis also suggested that a focus on the COVID-19 pandemic might have actually helped Republicans "by shifting Trump's rhetoric from immigration to fears around the economic impact of shutdowns, the virus gave conservative and low-information Latino voters a permission structure to back Trump even if they shunned him in 2016."[103]

Following the election, Biden pointed to Democratic messaging problems. These difficulties stemmed from an inability to properly respond to Republican accusations that Democrats wanted to "defund the police," a rallying cry adopted by some on the left in response to racial inequities in policing, which was a major focus of the campaign following the death of a Minneapolis Black man, George Floyd, at the hands of local police.[104] Democrats may have also been hurt by the fact that traditionally Republican voters who did not like Trump could vote against him in 2020 and split their tickets in favor of Republican House candidates—in 2018, the only way for voters to hurt Trump was to vote against his party's candidates down the ballot.

Overall, though, Democrats did maintain control of the chamber, and they did so without much of a margin in the overall House vote: they won about 51 percent of the votes cast for the House and converted that into about 51 percent of the total seats in the chamber. So for all of the talk of a Republican bias in the House earlier in the decade, Democrats in 2020 won a share of seats commensurate with their share of the national House vote for the second straight election.

As noted in the section on the election year of 2018, Democrats won the House majority by a wide enough margin to discount the unwinding of Republican gerrymanders in Florida and Virginia in 2016 and Pennsylvania in 2018. North Carolina's 2020 remap belongs on that list of favorable redistricting changes as well. However, given the small size of the Democrats' 2020 majority, it seems possible (if not likely) that the Republicans would have won the House in 2020 if no maps had changed throughout the decade. Political analyst J. Miles Coleman estimates that without the middecade redistricting in those four states, Republicans would have won roughly a half-dozen additional seats in 2020—enough to give them a very narrow majority.[105]

This was an unusual election in the sense that the winning White House party lost ground in the House, although that was not unprecedented. Four years earlier, Republicans lost ground in the House and the Senate while Trump was winning. Democrats also lost seats in 1992 when Bill Clinton beat George H. W. Bush, the last time a challenger had defeated an incumbent president. But as noted in the section on that election, redistricting helped Republicans that year; in 2020, the only changed maps, those in North Carolina, helped Democrats.

Perhaps a better historical precedent for 2020's House elections was an election conducted just before the time frame covered in this book: 1960. That year, John F. Kennedy defeated Richard M. Nixon in a highly competitive presidential election while Democrats lost 20 net seats in the House. Two years earlier, in 1958, Democrats had enjoyed one of their best years ever, netting 48 seats in the midst of a bad economy during President Dwight D. Eisenhower's second midterm. Democrats elected a big 283-seat majority that year, but they were unable to maintain it in the more competitive environment of 1960, which "seemed to mark the return to the GOP fold of traditionally Republican congressional districts, which had gone Democratic in 1958 as a temporary protest against GOP policies," a *Congressional Quarterly* history of the election noted.[106] Six decades later, this same description could apply to some of the turf that Republicans clawed back from Democrats following a disastrous midterm election two years earlier—both in districts Trump carried in places like Oklahoma City, Staten Island, and Charleston but also in traditionally Republican districts in South Florida and Southern California (even if Biden was carrying many of these districts at the presidential level). But in a testament to the Democrats' House strength in the middle of the last century, the party could sustain a 20-seat loss but still hold 263 seats. Meanwhile, a 13-seat loss in 2020 brought Democrats to the brink of losing their majority.

⊛ ⊛ ⊛

The slim Democratic House majority elected at the close of the decade was built on dominance in the Northeast and the West Coast, where Democrats won more than 75 percent of the seats combined. This allowed them to overcome deficits in the other three regions, as shown in figure 3.4, which tracks the Democrats' regional share of seats from 1996 to 2020. Democrats held just 42 percent of the seats in the Midwest, slightly less than a third in the Greater South, and barely over a third in the Interior West.

Figure 3.4. Regional share of House seats won by Democrats, 1996–2020

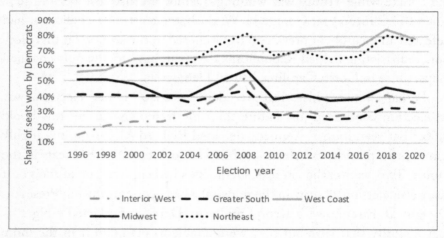

Source: Compiled by author

But as another redistricting and reapportionment cycle loomed, and as the poisoned chalice of holding the White House in a midterm cycle passed from Republican to Democratic hands, the Democrats' position in the House seemed highly vulnerable. They found themselves in such a position because, for the third straight presidential election and for the sixth time in eight presidential elections, the national House vote for Democrats lagged behind that of the Democratic presidential vote.

In the 1970s and 1980s, Democrats often lost presidential elections but maintained their House majorities even during those election years. In other words, their House candidates frequently ran ahead of their presidential candidates in presidential election years. Since the 1990s, Democratic presidential candidates have often performed better than Republican candidates: in the eight presidential elections from 1992 to 2020, Democrats won the Electoral College (and the presidency) five times, and they have won the national popular vote all but one time. But now they are the party whose House performance is likelier to lag behind their presidential showing. Figure 3.5 compares the Democratic share of the two-party presidential vote in presidential election years from 1972 to 2020 to the Democratic share of the adjusted two-party House vote in those same elections (the latter is the same calculation by Theodore Arrington that is cited in figure 3.2). Democrats ran well ahead of their presidential performance throughout the 1970s and 1980s, even in 1976, the one year in that timeframe when Democrats won the presidency. Since then, the Democratic share of the two-party House vote has often been lower than their two-party presidential share, including in 2012, 2016, and 2020. Even in a time of relatively meager ticket splitting, particularly compared to the 1970s and 1980s, there are still voters who do split their tickets, and that crossover voting has benefited House Republicans more than Democrats in recent presidential election years.

Figure 3.5. Democratic share of the adjusted two-party vote for House compared to two-party Democratic vote for president, 1972–2020

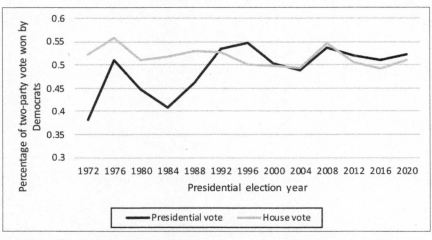

Source: House vote data calculated and provided by Theodore S. Arrington. Presidential vote data calculated by author from Dave Leip's Atlas of U.S. Presidential Elections (https://uselectionatlas.org/)

Losing US House seats was not the only down-ballot disappointment for Democrats in 2020. They also struck out on their state legislative targets, which had consequences for the post-2020 census redistricting process. Democrats hoped to gain a seat at the redistricting table in GOP-run states such as Georgia, North Carolina, and Texas, but Republicans held their state legislative majorities in all three states.[107] All told, and based on the 2020 census reapportionment of House seats, Republicans appeared to have the power to draw 187 districts and Democrats the power to draw 75, with another 167 being drawn either by nonpartisan commissions or by states under divided party control. The remaining 6 are in states with just a single House member.[108] The bottom line on 2022 redistricting was this: Republicans did not hold quite as much power as they did after the 2010 elections, but they still had more power than Democrats.

CONCLUSION

A Half Century of Change in the House

Although Democrats currently control the US House of Representatives, their majority is fragile. Thanks to gains in 2020, Republicans were well positioned to win the majority in 2022. They will once again wield more power in redistricting than Democrats and will likely benefit from re-apportionment. And if the 2022 midterm is anything like the previous four—2006, 2010, 2014, and 2018—a nationalized election that breaks against the White House could allow the GOP to net significantly more than the five seats they need to win control of the House.

For a variety of reasons, the House has transitioned from a body where Democratic control was a given throughout the 1960s, 1970s, and 1980s to one where the overall majority may be at least somewhat in doubt from election to election but where one might expect Republicans to win when national conditions favor them or in years where the electoral environment is more neutral.

However, it is also necessary to be humble when predicting the political future. As the long arc of this study should make clear, political coalitions are not necessarily static over time. It also may simply be that the House is at a point where regular changes are expected in the majority party as part of midterms where the party that does not hold the White House mobilizes in greater force than the more complacent presidential party. The last four midterms all broke decisively against the White House. The two before that, 1998 and 2002, were rare instances when the president's party gained seats at midterm, but both featured extraordinary circumstances: the Republicans' miscalculation in trying to impeach Clinton in the former, and the September 11 terrorist attacks and buildup to the Iraq War in the latter. It may have been that Democrats would have won the House in 2002 barring the jolting intrusion of terrorism and war (although, as noted in chapter 3, the Republicans had other emerging structural advantages in that election too). Going back a little further brings us to 1994, when the Democratic hammerlock on the House was finally loosened in the first place. However, it is possible that the House will both feature extreme volatility in the coming years and that Republicans also will enjoy a generic advantage in the midst of said volatility; these factors do not have to be mutually exclusive.

In order to hold the House in 2022, Democrats may need some of the unusual circumstances that allowed the presidential party to perform well in the 1998 and 2002 midterms. But as noted earlier, they seem unlikely to benefit from the decennial reapportionment and redistricting process, and that combined with midterm history suggests the Republicans should be well positioned to reclaim the House majority that they have usually held over the past three decades.

At the end of this history of House elections since the 1960s, it's worth looking at just how much has changed—or stayed the same—over the course of a half century. Every state had done something to comply with "one person, one vote" in advance of the 1968 election, and that election produced a 243–192 Democratic House. A half century later, voters restored the Democrats to a 235–200 majority in the House. While these two Houses separated by 50 years did not have the exact same partisan makeup, they were similar. And yet the building blocks of the Democratic majority were much different five decades ago than they are today.

In 1968, Democratic strength was built in the Greater South. The party held 75 percent of the seats in that region, and this majority was augmented by 58 percent of the seats from the Northeast and 59 percent from the West Coast. The heart of the Republican minority was in the Midwest, where they held 59 percent of the seats, and they held 80 percent of the seats in the Interior West, by far the most sparsely populated of the five regions.

By 2018 the Greater South had become overwhelmingly Republican. Democrats held only 33 percent of the seats in that region, and that was after netting 10 additional seats there in 2018. In other words, the Greater

South had gone from being the Democrats' strongest region to being its weakest. Democrats still held the Northeast and West Coast, and in greater force, with 80 percent of the seats in the former and 84 percent in the latter. The Midwest continued to be competitive but with a GOP tilt, as Republicans held 54 percent of the seats there, and they also held 59 percent of the seats in the Interior West. These trends in the percentage of seats won by Democrats in each region are shown for the entire period covered in this study, 1964–2020, in figure C.1.

Figure C.1. Regional share of House seats won by Democrats, 1964–2020

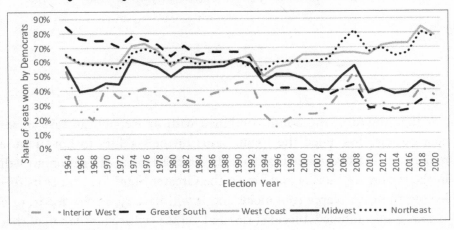

Source: Compiled by author

Reapportionment has made major changes to the regional distribution of power. In 1968 the Greater South held a plurality of the seats (29 percent), but it was followed closely by the Northeast (27 percent) and Midwest (26 percent). The West Coast (12 percent) and Interior West (7 percent) held less than one in five seats.

Let's now look at what has changed following the release of the 2020 census reapportionment figures in late April 2021.[1] Because of faster population growth, the Greater South now holds a much clearer plurality of the seats, more than one-third of the total (36 percent). The Northeast and Midwest both hold roughly one in five seats apiece, with the West Coast (16 percent) and Interior West (10 percent) now up to about a quarter of the seats combined. Figure C.2 shows the share of seats by region from the 1960 census through the 2020 census.

Figure C.2. Regional distribution of House seats, 1960 census to 2020 census

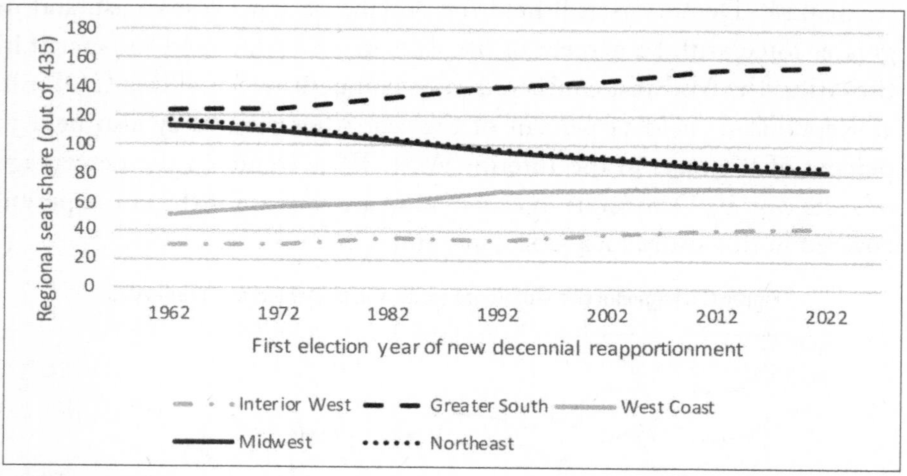

Source: Compiled by author

The growth of the South combined with its Republican turn in recent decades has aided the Republicans in their ability to hold House majorities. The two states that have driven the House delegation growth in the region are Florida and Texas. The Greater South had 124 seats following the 1960 reapportionment, and it will have 155 in the 2020s, or a 31-seat gain combined. Florida (+16) and Texas (+15) account for all of that growth; the other 12 states' changes net out to zero (although that obscures to some extent the growth in Georgia and North Carolina, which have added four and three seats, respectively, since the 1960s).

Between the two megastates of Florida and Texas, Democrats had a huge 29–6 House edge in 1968. By 2010, Republicans had a 42–15 edge in just the two states, although that had eroded slightly to a still-impressive 39–18 by 2020. Republicans, who currently rule both states, will have to grapple with adding seats but maintaining their control of the state delegations. The Republicans' usual strength in the Texas suburbs was tested in 2018, as they lost one seat apiece in suburban Dallas and Houston, and several other typically safe seats became much more competitive even though Republicans held them. One of the seats the Democrats captured in Texas was particularly symbolic: the suburban seat in Houston was TX-7, the descendant of a district created after the Reapportionment Revolution that George H. W. Bush carried, helping break what was at that time a Democratic monopoly in the Texas House delegation. Where once the suburbs provided a beachhead for Republican incursion in the South, they may now provide Democrats a path back to power in several states in the region. Yet Democrats stalled in Texas in 2020, showing an inability to pick up additional suburban territory or to capture a swing seat, TX-23, they had held earlier in the decade. Republicans in 2020 also won back the two seats they lost in South Florida in 2018.

While Democrats have shown some potential to win in the Greater South, Republicans still have a huge edge there. Of the 14 states there, Democrats are clearly ascendant in only Virginia, where they hold a majority of the US House delegation and majorities in both chambers of the state legislature. Republicans control majorities of the House seats and every single state legislative chamber in the other 13 states, although a breakthrough in Georgia in 2020—Democrats won the state for president and flipped two Senate seats in a pair of January 2021 runoff elections— gave the party hope there too.

Overall, there have been some hardening of partisan trends: the relatively smaller northeastern delegation and the relatively larger West Coast delegation have become more Democratic. This has allowed the Democrats to continue to compete with the Republicans at the House level.

However, the Greater South has become dramatically more Republican. The Midwest and Interior West are competitive with an overall Republican lean. And within many states there has been change as well. These changes have generally balanced out in the favor of Republicans, although as recently as the post-2010 reapportionment, the actual shifting of seats (somewhat surprisingly) did not seem to give the Republicans any advantage (although the shift following 2000 did).

As both parties reckon with the post-2020 census reapportionment and redistricting process, they will not have any new guidance from the US Supreme Court on how to draw the districts. In *Rucho v. Common Cause*, decided in June 2019, the Supreme Court, in a narrow majority decision, determined that it would not intervene in partisan redistricting cases. The court, of course, has never intervened in these partisan cases. So one way to look at the decision is that it really doesn't change anything; yet it's also possible that the court's decision represents a bright green light to both parties to redistrict even more aggressively than they have in the past. However, both parties remain constrained by possible court intervention against overly aggressive redistricting based on race, and reformers can turn to state courts to undo gerrymanders, as they did in Florida, North Carolina, and Pennsylvania in recent years. Of course, this is predicated on lawyers (or the courts themselves) finding something specific in state law that can be interpreted to allow intervention against aggressive gerrymanders. In North Carolina, the Democrats' six-to-one edge on the state supreme court was trimmed to a mere four-to-three advantage in 2020, and Republicans could retake that court in 2022. The Florida Supreme Court is also more conservative than it was in 2015—when it enforced the state's constitutional prohibitions on partisan gerrymandering—which may prompt it to defer to a Republican gerrymander despite the state's constitution.[2] It remains an open question how stridently both parties will redistrict in the places where they held sway; however, if both sides are maximally aggressive, Republicans will have more seats to work with than Democrats.

While this study covers nearly six decades of House elections and many of the major features of these elections, it is by no means complete. There are many individual results not covered here, including ones that many would find important and interesting. Also not covered in depth here are several aspects of the election process, such as the amount of money that goes into elections, the various ways in which this money is spent, and the rise of outside spending groups in House elections. Same goes for the demographics of the overall membership and the amount of turnover from year to year. This is also a work almost entirely devoted to elections as opposed to governance. Clearly, there is a lot one could analyze and discuss when it comes to the House.

Hopefully, this particular work augments the reams of written information about US House elections by detailing the House's electoral history over the 50-plus years since the Supreme Court's reapportionment decisions and exploring why a governing body that was dominated by Democrats is now not only competitive but also, at least to some degree, Republican leaning.

Notes

Foreword

1 Richard M. Scammon and Ben J. Wattenberg, *The Real Majority: An Extraordinary Examination of the American Electorate* (New York: Coward-McCann, 1970).

Introduction

1 John F. Harris, *The Survivor: Bill Clinton in the White House* (New York: Random House, 2006), 150.
2 Prior to the ratification of the 20th Amendment in 1935, a newly elected House would not convene until December of the following year. So, in this instance, the House elected in 1930 did not meet for the first time until December 1931, allowing party control to flip from Republican to Democratic because of special elections. The 20th Amendment set the current calendar, with the newly elected Congress meeting on January 3, or another date specified by Congress, following the previous November's election. See Edward J. Larson and Jeff Shesol, "Common Interpretation: The Twentieth Amendment," National Constitution Center, https://constitutioncenter.org/interactive-constitution/interpretation/amendment-xx/interps/153.
3 Sam Rosenfeld, *The Polarizers: Postwar Architects of Our Partisan Era* (Chicago: University of Chicago Press, 2018), 3.
4 Frances E. Lee, *Insecure Majorities: Congress and the Perpetual Campaign* (Chicago: University of Chicago Press, 2016).
5 Rosenfeld, *Polarizers,* 3.
6 James M. Curry and Frances E. Lee, *The Limits of Party: Congress and Lawmaking in a Polarized Era* (Chicago: University of Chicago Press, 2020).

Data, Definitions, and Methodology

1 David A. Hopkins, *Red Fighting Blue: How Geography and Electoral Rules Polarize American Politics* (New York: Cambridge University Press, 2017), 26.

2 Hopkins, *Red Fighting Blue,* 27.

3 Linda Qiu, "Is Bernie Sanders a Democrat?," PolitiFact, February 23, 2016, https://www.politifact.com/article/2016/feb/23/bernie-sanders-democrat/.

4 Robert V. Remini, *The House: The History of the House of Representatives* (Washington, DC: Smithsonian Books, 2007), 282.

CHAPTER 1: THE PARTISAN CONSEQUENCES OF THE REAPPORTIONMENT REVOLUTION IN THE UNITED STATES HOUSE OF REPRESENTATIVES, 1964–74

1 "The Governor's Vetoes," *New York Times,* May 29, 1965, https://www.nytimes.com/1965/05/29/archives/the-governors-vetoes.html.

2 Erik J. Engstrom, *Partisan Gerrymandering and the Construction of American Democracy* (Ann Arbor: University of Michigan Press, 2013), 8.

3 Andrew Hacker, *Congressional Districting: The Issue of Equal Representation* (Washington, DC: Brookings Institution, 1963), 2.

4 Hacker, 2.

5 Hacker, 3.

6 Mark Monmonier, *Bushmanders and Bullwinkles: How Politicians Manipulate Electronic Maps and Census Data to Win Elections* (Chicago: University of Chicago Press, 2001), 1.

7 Mark E. Rush, *Does Redistricting Make a Difference? Partisan Representation and Electoral Behavior* (Baltimore: Johns Hopkins University Press, 1993), 2.

8 Elmer C. Griffith, *The Rise and Development of the Gerrymander* (Chicago: Scott, Foresman, 1907), 26–29.

9 Thomas E. Mann, "Redistricting Reform: What Is Desirable? Possible?," in *Party Lines: Competition, Partisanship, and Congressional Redistricting,* ed. Thomas E. Mann and Bruce E. Cain (Washington, DC: Brookings Institution, 2005), 111. Political scientist Thomas Rogers Hunter disputes the idea that Madison's district was gerrymandered, arguing that the district was compactly drawn and only seemed gerrymandered because Madison lived in an anti-Federalist area. See Thomas Rogers Hunter, "The First Gerrymander? Patrick Henry, James Madison, James Monroe, and Virginia's 1788 Congressional Districting," *Early American Studies: An Interdisciplinary Journal* 9, no. 3 (Fall 2011): 781.

10 Engstrom, *Partisan Gerrymandering,* 8.

11 Engstrom, 9.

12 Engstrom, 177.

13 Engstrom, 172.

14 J. Douglas Smith, *On Democracy's Doorstep: The Inside Story of How the Supreme Court Brought "One Person, One Vote" to the United States* (New York: Hill and Wang, 2014), 18.

15 Engstrom, *Partisan Gerrymandering,* 152–54.

16 Smith, *On Democracy's Doorstep,* 50.

17 Colegrove v. Green, 328 U.S. 549 (1946).

18 Wesberry v. Sanders, 376 U.S. 1 (1964).

19 Stephen Ansolabehere and James M. Snyder Jr., *The End of Inequality: One Person, One Vote and the Transformation of American Politics* (New York: W. W. Norton, 2008), 95.

20 Charles S. Bullock III, *Redistricting: The Most Political Activity in America,* 2nd ed. (Lanham, MD: Rowman & Littlefield, 2021), 58.

21 Bullock, 46.

22 Carl Hulse, "Colorado Court Rejects Redistricting Plan," *New York Times,* December 2, 2003, https://www.nytimes.com/2003/12/02/us/colorado-court-rejects-redistricting-plan.html.

23 Smith, *On Democracy's Doorstep,* 283–84.

24 David R. Mayhew, "Congressional Representation: Theory and Practice in Drawing the Districts," in *Reapportionment in the 1970s,* ed. Nelson W. Polsby (Berkeley: University of California Press, 1971), 277.

25 Nathaniel Persily, Thad Kousser, and Patrick Egan, "The Complicated Impact of One Person, One Vote on Political Competition and Representation," *North Carolina Law Review* 80, no. 4 (2002): 1326.

26 Robert J. Sickels, "Dragons, Bacon Strips and Dumbbells—Who's Afraid of Reapportionment?," *Yale Law Journal* 75, no. 8 (July 1966): 1308.

27 Robert S. Erikson, "Malapportionment, Gerrymandering, and Party Fortunes in Congressional Elections," *American Political Science Review* 66, no. 4 (December 1972): 1243.

28 Charles Backstrom, Samuel Krislov, and Leonard Robins, "Desperately Seeking Standards: The Court's Frustrating Attempts to Limit Political Gerrymandering." *PS: Political Science and Politics* 39, no. 3 (July 2006): 409–10.

29 Rucho v. Common Cause, 139 U.S. 2484 (2019).

30 Gary W. Cox and Jonathan N. Katz, "The Reapportionment Revolution and Bias in U. S. Congressional Elections." *American Journal of Political Science* 43, no. 3 (July 1999): 812.

31 Gary W. Cox and Jonathan N. Katz, *Elbridge Gerry's Salamander: The Electoral Consequences of the Reapportionment Revolution* (New York: Cambridge University Press, 2002), 24.

32 Ward Elliott, "Prometheus, Proteus, Pandora, and Procrustes Unbound: The Political Consequences of Reapportionment." *University of Chicago Law Review* 37, no. 3 (Spring 1970): 489.

33 Seth C. McKee, *Republican Ascendancy in Southern U.S. House Elections* (Boulder, CO: Westview, 2010), 17.

34 McKee, 17.

35 David Lublin, *The Republican South: Democratization and Partisan Change* (Princeton, NJ: Princeton University Press, 2004), 22.

36 McKee, 53.

37 McKee, 72.

38 Nicol C. Rae, *The Decline and Fall of the Liberal Republicans from 1952 to the Present* (New York: Oxford University Press, 1989), 159.

39 Mark C. Shelley II, *The Permanent Majority: The Conservative Coalition in the United States Congress* (Tuscaloosa: University of Alabama Press, 1983), 35.

40 David A. Hopkins, *Red Fighting Blue: How Geography and Electoral Rules Polarize American Politics* (New York: Cambridge University Press, 2017), 102.

41 Cox and Katz, "Reapportionment Revolution and Bias in U.S. Congressional Elections," 812.

42 Cox and Katz, 819.

43 Milton C. Cummings Jr., "Reapportionment in the 1970s: Its Effects on Congress," in *Reapportionment in the 1970s*, ed. Nelson W. Polsby (Berkeley: University of California Press, 1971), 210–211, 221.

44 Kenneth C. Martis, *The Historical Atlas of United States Congressional Districts, 1789–1983* (New York: Free Press, 1982), 218.

45 Michael Barone, Grant Ujifusa, and Douglas Matthews, *The Almanac of American Politics 1972* (Boston: Gambit, 1972), 422.

46 Andrew E. Busch, *Horses in Midstream: U.S. Midterm Elections and Their Consequences, 1894–1998* (Pittsburgh, PA: University of Pittsburgh Press, 1999), 9.

47 Busch, 100–101.

48 "Albert Watson, 72, Lawmaker; Opposed Integration of Schools," *New York Times*, September 27, 1994, https://www.nytimes.com/1994/09/27/obituaries/albert -watson-72-lawmaker-opposed-integration-of-schools.html.

49 Timothy P. Nokken and Keith T. Poole, "Congressional Party Defection in American History," *Legislative Studies Quarterly* 29, no. 4 (November 2004): 555.

50 Sean Trende, *The Lost Majority: Why the Future of Government Is Up for Grabs— and Who Will Take It* (New York: Palgrave Macmillan, 2012), 27.

51 Smith, *On Democracy's Doorstep*, 277.

52 Jay K. Dow, *Electing the House: The Adoption and Performance of the US Single-Member District Electoral System* (Lawrence: University Press of Kansas, 2017), 186.

53 Barone, Ujifusa, and Matthews, *Almanac of American Politics 1972*, 504–6.

54 Earl Caldwell, "3 Negroes Weigh House Race in New Brooklyn 12th District," *New York Times*, February 26, 1968, https://www.nytimes.com/1968/02/26 /archives/3-negroes-weigh-house-race-in-new-brooklyn-12th-district .html?searchResultPosition=1.

55 Erikson, "Malapportionment, Gerrymandering, and Party Fortunes," 1242.

56 Barone, Ujifusa, and Matthews, *Almanac of American Politics 1972*, 593.

57 Barone, Ujifusa, and Matthews, 754.

58 Barone, Ujifusa, and Matthews, 410.

59 "California Takes Population Lead," *New York Times*, September 1, 1964, https://www.nytimes.com/1964/09/01/archives/california-takes-population-lead-but-new-york-is-still-ahead-in.html.

60 Sidney E. Zion, "State Republicans See a Gain of 6 to 8 House Seats," *New York Times*, April 8, 1969, https://www.nytimes.com/1969/04/08/archives/state-republicans-see-a-gain-of-6-to-8-house-seats.html?searchResultPosition=1.

61 Barone, Ujifusa, and Matthews, *Almanac of American Politics 1972*, 510.

62 Barone, Ujifusa, and Matthews, 543.

63 Robert M. Rogers, "Illinois Redistricting History Since 1970," Illinois General Assembly Research Response, May 28, 2008, http://www.ilga.gov/commission/lru/28.RedistrictingSince1970.pdf.

64 "House: Republican Gain of 12, New Count of 244–191," in *CQ Almanac 1972*, 28th ed. (Washington, DC: Congressional Quarterly, 1973), 1020–32, http://library.cqpress.com/cqalmanac/cqal72-1249887.

65 Michael Barone, Grant Ujifusa, and Douglas Matthews, *The Almanac of American Politics 1974* (Boston: Gambit, 1973), 177.

66 Barone, Ujifusa, and Matthews, *Almanac of American Politics 1974*, 951.

67 Barone, Ujifusa, and Matthews, 974.

68 Barone, Ujifusa, and Matthews, 462–63.

69 Steven V. Roberts, "House Censures Crane and Studds for Sexual Relations with Pages," *New York Times*, July 21, 1983, https://www.nytimes.com/1983/07/21/us/house-censures-crane-and-studds-for-sexual-relations-with-pages.html?searchResultPosition=1.

70 Barone, Ujifusa, and Matthews, *Almanac of American Politics 1974*, 160–61.

71 Barone, Ujifusa, and Matthews, 393.

72 Barone, Ujifusa, and Matthews, 545.

73 Barone, Ujifusa, and Matthews, 1002–3.

74 Barone, Ujifusa, and Matthews, 1042.

75 Barone, Ujifusa, and Matthews, 926.

76 Amihai Glazer, Bernard Grofman, and Marc Robbins, "Partisan and Incumbency Effects of 1970s Congressional Redistricting," *American Journal of Political Science* 31, no. 3 (August 1987): 680.

77 Greg Giroux, "U.S. House Special Elections, 1957–Present," Google Document, https://docs.google.com/spreadsheets/d/1DX4nvZ32rOQeU6B-zc_khCFg7b35ezeXtJYG3bIOUDo/edit#gid=0.

78 David R. Smith and Thomas L. Brunell, "Special Elections to the U.S. House of Representatives: A General Election Barometer?," *Legislative Studies Quarterly* 35, no. 2 (May 2010): 293.

79 Busch, *Horses in Midstream*, 33.

80 Busch, 36.

81 Richard E. Cohen with James A. Barnes, *The Almanac of American Politics 2016* (Bethesda, MD: Columbia, 2015), 937.

82 White v. Weiser, 412 U.S. 783 (1973).

83 Michael Barone, Grant Ujifusa, and Douglas Matthews, *The Almanac of American Politics 1976* (New York: E. P. Dutton, 1975), 263.

84 Barone, Ujifusa, and Matthews, *Almanac of American Politics 1976*, 170–71.

85 Barone, Ujifusa, and Matthews, 338.

CHAPTER 2: THE ROOTS OF THE REPUBLICAN REVOLUTION

1 William F. Connelly Jr., and John J. Pitney Jr., *Congress' Permanent Minority? Republicans in the U.S. House* (Lanham, MD: Rowman and Littlefield, 1994).

2 David Lublin, *The Republican South: Democratization and Partisan Change* (Princeton, NJ: Princeton University Press, 2004), 6.

3 Nicol C. Rae, *Southern Democrats* (New York: Oxford University Press, 1994), 3.

4 Rae, 23.

5 Gary C. Jacobson, *The Electoral Origins of Divided Government: Competition in U.S. House Elections, 1946–1988* (Boulder, CO: Westview, 1990), 133.

6 Jacobson, 62.

7 Lublin, *Republican South*, 18.

8 Frances E. Lee, *Insecure Majorities: Congress and the Perpetual Campaign* (Chicago: University of Chicago Press, 2016), 12.

9 Alan I. Abramowitz, "Partisan Redistricting and the 1982 Congressional Elections," *Journal of Politics* 45, no. 3 (August 1983): 770.

10 Ann Devroy, "Bush to Propose Outlawing Gerrymandering," *Washington Post*, June 28, 1989, https://www.washingtonpost.com/archive/politics/1989/06/28/bush-to-propose-outlawing-gerrymandering/off3b1bb-88f4-4947-8ea6-ac4835a54b21/.

11 The US Supreme Court later gutted the Voting Rights Act's section 5 preclearance coverage formula in the 2013 decision Shelby County v. Holder. As of this writing, Congress had not established a new formula for determining which jurisdictions should be subject to preclearance.

12 Maurice T. Cunningham, *Maximization, Whatever the Cost: Race, Redistricting, and the Department of Justice* (Westport, CT: Praeger, 2001), 6.

13 Cunningham, 43.

14 David T. Canon, *Race, Redistricting, and Representation: The Unintended Consequences of Black Majority Districts* (Chicago: University of Chicago Press, 1999), 12.

15 Cunningham, *Maximization, Whatever the Cost*, 6.

16 Lublin, *Republican South*, 112.

17 Jacobson, *Electoral Origins of Divided Government*, 119.

18 Jacobson, 133.

19 Thomas E. Mann, "Is the House of Representatives Unresponsive to Political Change?," in *Elections American Style*, ed. A. James Reichley (Washington, DC: Brookings Institution, 1987), 277.

20 Andrew E. Busch, *Horses in Midstream: U.S. Midterm Elections and Their Consequences, 1894–1998* (Pittsburgh, PA: University of Pittsburgh Press, 1999), 22.

21 Robert S. Erikson, "Why the Democrats Lose Presidential Elections: Toward a Theory of Optimal Loss," *PS: Political Science and Politics* 22, no. 1 (March 1989): 31.

22 William Safire, "Dishing the Whigs," *New York Times*, November 9, 1978, https://www.nytimes.com/1978/11/09/archives/essay-dishing-the-whigs.html?searchResultPosition=1.

23 *Congressional Elections 1946–1996, Congressional Quarterly* (Washington, DC: Congressional Quarterly, 1998), 39.

24 Busch, *Horses in Midstream*, 107.

25 Sarah Lyall, "In Redrawn District, What Went Wrong for Green in Election," *New York Times*, November 10, 1992, https://www.nytimes.com/1992/11/10/nyregion/in-redrawn-district-what-went-wrong-for-green-in-election.html.

26 Mark C. Shelley II, *The Permanent Majority: The Conservative Coalition in the United States Congress* (Tuscaloosa: University of Alabama Press, 1983), 160–61.

27 Michael Barone and Grant Ujifusa, *The Almanac of American Politics 1982* (Washington, DC: Barone, 1981), xxxv.

28 Margot Hornblower and T. R. Reid, "After Two Decades, the 'Boll Weevils' Are Back, and Whistling Dixie," *Washington Post*, April 26, 1981, https://www.washingtonpost.com/archive/politics/1981/04/26/after-two-decades-the-boll-weevils-are-back-and-whistling-dixie/c256b8cd-840f-4ce9-bec3-790e832e7e84/.

29 Mikva and Nolan share an unusual similarity. Both served nonconsecutive stints in the House and both served in different districts during those two stints. Mikva served in IL-2 from 1969 to 1973 and decided to run in IL-10 in 1972. He lost in 1972 but won in 1974, and he served until 1979, when President Carter appointed him to an appellate judgeship (he later served as President Clinton's White House counsel). Nolan represented MN-6 from 1975 to 1981 and then returned three decades later in a northeastern Minnesota seat covering the state's Iron Range, MN-8. He won three competitive elections in 2012, 2014, and 2016 before opting not to run again in 2018.

30 Barone and Ujifusa, *Almanac of American Politics 1982*, 354.

31 Myrna Oliver, "James C. Corman; 10-Term Valley Congressman Championed Civil Rights, Welfare Legislation," *Los Angeles Times*, January 3, 2001, https://www.latimes.com/archives/la-xpm-2001-jan-03-me-7825-story.html.

32 Ted Sherman, "Jersey Hustle: The Real-Life Story of Abscam," NJ.com, November 25, 2013, https://www.nj.com/inside-jersey/2013/11/jersey_hustle_the_real-life_story_of_abscam.html.

33 Lee, *Insecure Majorities*, 91.

34 Douglas B. Harris, "Legislative Parties and Leadership Choice: Confrontation or Accommodation in the 1989 Gingrich-Madigan Whip Race," *American Politics Research* 34, no. 2 (March 2006): 189–222.

35 Julian E. Zelizer, *Burning Down the House: Newt Gingrich, the Fall of a Speaker, and the Rise of the New Republican Party* (New York: Penguin, 2020), 50.

36 Busch, *Horses in Midstream*, 127.

37 Michael Barone, *Our Country: The Shaping of America from Roosevelt to Reagan* (New York: Free Press, 1990), 625.

38 Abramowitz, "Partisan Redistricting and the 1982 Congressional Elections," 770.

39 Michael Barone and Grant Ujifusa, *The Almanac of American Politics 1984* (Washington, DC: National Journal, 1983), 73–74.

40 Christopher Buchanan, "Classic Gerrymander by Indiana Republicans," *Congressional Quarterly Weekly Report*, October 17, 1981, 2017–22.

41 John T. Martin, "Former 8th District Rep. Joel Deckard Dies," *Courier & Press*, September 8, 2016, https://www.courierpress.com/story/news/local/2016/09/08/former-8th-district-rep-joel-deckard-dies/89999810/.

42 David Rogers, "Indiana's 'Bloody Eighth' District Shows Congressional-Race Tactics," *Wall Street Journal*, September 13, 2000, https://www.wsj.com/articles/SB968798191446556778.

43 Barone and Ujifusa, *Almanac of American Politics 1984*, 326.

44 Barone and Ujifusa, 935–36.

45 Tim Sablik, "Recession of 1981–82," Federal Reserve History, November 22, 2013, https://www.federalreservehistory.org/essays/recession_of_1981_82.

46 Gary C. Jacobson and Jamie L. Carson, *The Politics of Congressional Elections*, 10th ed. (Lanham, MD: Rowman and Littlefield, 2020), 215.

47 Jacobson and Carson, *Politics of Congressional Elections*, 73.

48 Busch, *Horses in Midstream*, 129–30.

49 Michael Barone and Grant Ujifusa, *The Almanac of American Politics 1986* (Washington, DC: National Journal, 1985), 1281.

50 Barone and Ujifusa, 862.

51 Barone and Ujifusa, *Almanac of American Politics 1984*, 868.

52 Robert Pear, "The 1992 Campaign: Congressional Districts; Redistricting Expected to Bring Surge in Minority Lawmakers," *New York Times*, August 3, 1992, https://www.nytimes.com/1992/08/03/us/1992-campaign-congressional-districts-redistricting-expected-bring-surge.html?searchResultPosition=1.

53 Zelizer, *Burning Down the House*, 78–84.

54 Larry J. Sabato, Kyle Kondik, and Geoffrey Skelley, "16 for '16: Bite-Sized Observations on a Wild Election," *Sabato's Crystal Ball*, November 17, 2016, http://www.centerforpolitics.org/crystalball/articles/16-for-16/.

55 Zelizer, *Burning Down the House*, 295.

56 Reid Wilson, "Pioneer of Modern Redistricting Dies at 75," *The Hill*, August 18, 2018, http://thehill.com/homenews/state-watch/402489-pioneer-of-modern-redistricting-dies-at-75.

57 Michael Barone and Grant Ujifusa, *The Almanac of American Politics 1994* (Washington, DC: National Journal, 1993), xl.

58 Barone and Ujifusa, 1209.

59 Barone and Ujifusa, xl.

60 Cunningham, *Maximization, Whatever the Cost*, 6.

61 David Lublin, *The Paradox of Representation: Racial Gerrymandering and Minority Interests in Congress* (Princeton, NJ: Princeton University Press, 1997), 23.

62 Barone and Ujifusa, *Almanac of American Politics 1994*, 285.

63 Barone and Ujifusa, 21.

64 Barone and Ujifusa, 331.

65 Kyle Kondik, "Open Season in the House," *Sabato's Crystal Ball*, January 18, 2018, http://www.centerforpolitics.org/crystalball/articles/open-season-in-the-house/.

66 Michael A. Dimock and Gary C. Jacobson, "Checks and Choices: The House Bank Scandal's Impact on Voters in 1992." *Journal of Politics* 57, no. 4 (November 1995): 1143.

67 Dimock and Jacobson, 1143.

68 Dimock and Jacobson, 1143.

69 Michael Lyons and Peter F. Galderisi, "Incumbency, Reapportionment, and U.S. House Redistricting," *Political Research Quarterly* 48, no. 4 (December 1995): 864.

70 Lee, *Insecure Majorities*, 105.

71 Steve Kornacki, *The Red and the Blue: The 1990s and the Birth of Political Tribalism* (New York: HarperCollins, 2018), 244–45.

72 Robert V. Remini, *The House: The History of the House of Representatives* (Washington, DC: Smithsonian Books, 2007), 480–81.

73 "How Trump Compares with Past Presidents: Bill Clinton," FiveThirtyEight, https://projects.fivethirtyeight.com/trump-approval-ratings/.

74 Barone and Ujifusa, *Almanac of American Politics 1994*, xl.

75 Kornacki, *Red and the Blue*, 274.

76 R. W. Apple Jr., "The 1994 Elections: Congress—News Analysis: How Lasting a Majority? Despite Sweeping Gains for Republicans, History Suggests the Power Is Temporary," *New York Times*, November 10, 1994, https://

www.nytimes.com/1994/11/10/us/1994-elections-congress-analysis-lasting
-majority-despite-sweeping-gains-for.html?searchResultPosition=6.

CHAPTER 3: THE HOUSE FROM 1996 TO 2020

1 Technically, Republicans narrowly won the House majority in the 1930 midterm. But by the time the House met for its first session in December 1931,
Democrats had a slight edge thanks to a series of special-election victories
throughout 1931. For the purposes of this calculation average, we are counting
the November 1930 results.

2 Theodore S. Arrington, "Seats/Votes Relationship in the U.S. House 1972–
2020," *Sabato's Crystal Ball,* February 4, 2021, https://centerforpolitics.org
/crystalball/articles/seats-votes-relationship-in-the-u-s-house-1972-2020/.

3 Nicholas O. Stephanopoulos and Eric M. McGhee, "Partisan Gerrymandering
and the Efficiency Gap," *University of Chicago Law Review* 82, no. 2 (March
2015): 852.

4 Stephanopoulos and McGhee, 871.

5 Samuel Issacharoff, "Gerrymandering and Political Cartels," *Harvard Law Review* 116, no. 2 (December 2002): 634.

6 Richard E. Cohen with James A. Barnes, *The Almanac of American Politics 2018*
(Bethesda, MD: Columbia, 2017), 1429.

7 Issacharoff, "Gerrymandering and Political Cartels," 636.

8 Christian R. Grose, *Congress in Black and White: Race and Representation in
Washington and at Home* (New York: Cambridge University Press, 2011), 46.

9 Grose, 45.

10 D. Stephen Voss and David Lublin, "Black Incumbents, White Districts: An
Appraisal of the 1996 Congressional Elections," *American Politics Research* 29,
no. 2 (March 2001): 141–82.

11 Michael Li and Laura Royden, "Minority Representation: No Conflict with
Fair Maps," Brennan Center for Justice, September 5, 2017, https://www
.brennancenter.org/our-work/research-reports/minority-representation-no
-conflict-fair-maps.

12 Mark E. Rush, *Does Redistricting Make a Difference? Partisan Representation and
Electoral Behavior* (Baltimore: Johns Hopkins University Press, 1993), 9.

13 Andrew Gelman and Gary King, "Enhancing Democracy through Legislative
Redistricting," *American Political Science Review* 88, no. 3 (September 1994): 541.

14 Kyle Kondik, "The House: Unclear Lines, Clear Expectations," *Sabato's Crystal Ball,* March 25, 2021, https://centerforpolitics.org/crystalball/articles/the
-house-unclear-lines-clear-expectations/.

15 Bernard Grofman and Thomas L. Brunell, "The Art of the Dummymander: The
Impact of Recent Redistrictings on the Partisan Makeup of Southern House

Seats," in *Redistricting in the New Millennium*, ed. Peter F. Galderisi (Lanham, MD: Lexington, 2005), 184.

16 Rush, *Does Redistricting Make a Difference?*, 141–42.

17 Nicholas R. Seabrook, *Drawing the Lines: Constraints on Partisan Gerrymandering in U.S. Politics* (Ithaca, NY: Cornell University Press, 2017), 121.

18 Thomas E. Mann, "Redistricting Reform: What Is Desirable? Possible?," in *Party Lines: Competition, Partisanship, and Congressional Redistricting*, ed. Thomas E. Mann and Bruce E. Cain (Washington, DC: Brookings Institution, 2005), 108.

19 Anthony J. McGann, Charles Anthony Smith, Michael Latner, and Alex Keena, *Gerrymandering in America: The House of Representatives, the Supreme Court, and the Future of Popular Sovereignty* (New York: Cambridge University Press, 2016), 225.

20 McGann et al., 18.

21 Sam Wang, "The Great Gerrymander of 2012," *New York Times*, February 2, 2013, http://www.nytimes.com/2013/02/03/opinion/sunday/the-great-gerrymander -of-2012.html?pagewanted=all&_r=0.

22 Clare Foran and Annie Grayer, "House Passes Sweeping Election Bill That Would Counter GOP Efforts to Restrict Voter Access," CNN, March 4, 2021, https://www.cnn.com/2021/03/03/politics/house-democrats-hr1-vote/index .html.

23 Jonathan A. Rodden, *Why Cities Lose: The Deep Roots of the Urban-Rural Political Divide* (New York: Basic Books, 2019), 3.

24 "Exit Polls," CNN, November 10, 2020, https://www.cnn.com/election/2020 /exit-polls/president/national-results.

25 McGann et al., *Gerrymandering in America*, 107.

26 Alan I. Abramowitz and Steven Webster, "The Rise of Negative Partisanship and the Nationalization of U.S. Elections in the 21st Century," *Electoral Studies: An International Journal* 41 (March 2016): 12.

27 Alan I. Abramowitz, "Moderation in the Pursuit of Victory May Not Help: Evidence from U.S. House Elections, 1978–2018" (paper presented at the Annual Meeting of the American Political Science Association, Marriott Wardman Park Hotel, Washington, DC, August 29–September 2, 2019).

28 Gary C. Jacobson, "It's Nothing Personal: The Decline of the Incumbency Advantage in US House Elections," *Journal of Politics* 77, no. 3 (July 2015): 861.

29 Gary C. Jacobson, "Extreme Referendum: Donald Trump and the 2018 Midterm Elections," *Political Science Quarterly* 134, no. 1 (Spring 2019): 24.

30 Jeffrey M. Stonecash, *Interpreting Congressional Elections: The Curious Case of the Incumbency Effect* (New York: Routledge, 2018), 58–59.

31 John Sides and Eric McGhee, "Redistricting Didn't Win Republicans the House," *Washington Post*, February 17, 2013, https://www

.washingtonpost.com/news/wonk/wp/2013/02/17/redistricting-didnt-win
-republicans-the-house/?utm_term=.16d635b6e426.

32 Michael Barone and Grant Ujifusa, *The Almanac of American Politics 1998* (Washington, DC: National Journal, 1997), 608.

33 Barone and Ujifusa, 1062–1063.

34 Portions of this section dealing with the 1998 election were previously published by the author in "The Shadow of 1998," *Sabato's Crystal Ball*, June 6, 2019, http://centerforpolitics.org/crystalball/articles/the-shadow-of-1998/.

35 Michael Tomasky, *Bill Clinton* (New York: Times, 2017), 118.

36 "How Trump Compares with Past Presidents: Bill Clinton," FiveThirtyEight, https://projects.fivethirtyeight.com/trump-approval-ratings/.

37 Tomasky, *Bill Clinton*, 118.

38 Michael Barone and Grant Ujifusa, *The Almanac of American Politics 2000* (Washington, DC: National Journal, 1999), 1059.

39 Barone and Ujifusa, 1681.

40 Barone and Ujifusa, 1389.

41 Barone and Ujifusa, 680.

42 Ceci Connolly and Howard Kurtz, "Gingrich Orchestrated GOP Ads Recalling Clinton-Lewinsky Affair," *Washington Post*, October 30, 1998, https://www.washingtonpost.com/wp-srv/politics/special/clinton/stories/ads103098.htm.

43 Barone and Ujifusa, *Almanac of American Politics 2000*, 362.

44 David E. Rosenbaum, "The 1998 Campaign: Indiana; District May Be a Barometer, Thanks to a Tight Race and Early Results," *New York Times*, October 30, 1998, https://www.nytimes.com/1998/10/30/us/1998-campaign-indiana-district-may-be-barometer-thanks-tight-race-early-results.html.

45 "Observers Say Residency Issue Sunk Gejdenson," Associated Press, November 13, 2000, https://www.middletownpress.com/news/article/Observers-say-residency-issue-sunk-Gejdenson-11939333.php.

46 Michael Barone with Richard E. Cohen, *The Almanac of American Politics 2002* (Washington, DC: National Journal, 2001), 1535.

47 Larry J. Sabato, "The George W. Bush Midterm," in *Midterm Madness: The Elections of 2002*, ed. Larry J. Sabato (Lanham, MD: Rowman and Littlefield, 2003), 9–10.

48 "Presidential Approval Ratings—George W. Bush," Gallup, https://news.gallup.com/poll/116500/presidential-approval-ratings-george-bush.aspx.

49 Richard G. Niemi and Alan I. Abramowitz, "Partisan Redistricting and the 1992 Congressional Elections," *Journal of Politics* 56, no. 3 (August 1994): 813.

50 Glen Bolger and Jim Hobart, "Why the GOP Could Keep the House in 2012," *Sabato's Crystal Ball*, April 14, 2011, http://centerforpolitics.org/crystalball/articles/gxb2011041402/.

51 Michael Barone with Richard E. Cohen, *The Almanac of American Politics 2004* (Washington, DC: National Journal, 2003), 54–55.

52 Barone and Cohen, 454.

53 Barone and Cohen, 401.

54 Barone and Cohen, 44–45.

55 Barone and Cohen, 1510–11.

56 Brian Beutler, "Flashback: Texas Dems Fled State in 2003 to Block GOP Re-redistricting Plan," Talking Points Memo, February 17, 2011, https://talkingpointsmemo.com/dc/flashback-texas-dems-fled-state-in-2003-to-block-gop-re-redistricting-plan.

57 William A. Galston, "Why the 2005 Social Security Initiative Failed, and What It Means for the Future," Brookings Institution, September 21, 2007, https://www.brookings.edu/research/why-the-2005-social-security-initiative-failed-and-what-it-means-for-the-future/.

58 "Presidential Approval Ratings—George W. Bush," Gallup, https://news.gallup.com/poll/116500/presidential-approval-ratings-george-bush.aspx.

59 Michael Barone with Richard E. Cohen, *The Almanac of American Politics 2008* (Washington, DC: National Journal, 2007), 1494.

60 Barone and Cohen, 29.

61 Naftali Bendavid, "The House Rahm Built," *Chicago Tribune,* November 12, 2006, https://www.chicagotribune.com/politics/chi-0611120215nov12-story.html.

62 Barone and Cohen, *Almanac of American Politics 2008,* 30.

63 David Wasserman, "The 2006 House Midterm Maelstrom," in *The Sixth Year Itch: The Rise and Fall of the George W. Bush Presidency,* ed. Larry J. Sabato (New York: Pearson Longman, 2008), 117–20.

64 Wasserman, 114.

65 "Congressman Apologizes for Affair in TV Ad," *Associated Press,* October 4, 2006, http://www.nbcnews.com/id/15132240/ns/politics/t/congressman-apologizes-affair-tv-ad/#.XSPXUuhKjct.

66 Charles S. Bullock III, *Redistricting: The Most Political Activity in America,* 2nd ed. (Lanham, MD: Rowman & Littlefield, 2021), 194–96.

67 Barone and Cohen, *Almanac of American Politics 2008,* 29.

68 Stuart Rothenberg, "April Madness: Can GOP Win Back the House in 2010?," *Roll Call,* April 22, 2009, https://www.rollcall.com/2009/04/22/april-madness-can-gop-win-back-the-house-in-2010/.

69 Kyle Kondik, "The Politics of the Shutdown," *Sabato's Crystal Ball,* October 3, 2013, http://centerforpolitics.org/crystalball/articles/the-politics-of-the-shutdown/.

70 John M. Broder, "House Passes Bill to Address Threat of Climate Change," *New York Times,* June 26, 2009, https://www.nytimes.com/2009/06/27/us/politics/27climate.html.

71 Liz Hamel et al., "5 Charts about Public Opinion on the Affordable Care Act and the Supreme Court," Kaiser Family Foundation, December 18, 2020, https://www.kff.org/health-reform/poll-finding/5-charts-about-public-opinion-on-the-affordable-care-act-and-the-supreme-court/.

72 Kondik, "Politics of the Shutdown."

73 John Sides, "Health Care Reform Counterfactuals," Monkey Cage, March 9, 2012, http://themonkeycage.org/2012/03/health-care-reform-counterfactuals/.

74 Bolger and Hobart, "Why the GOP Could Keep the House in 2012."

75 Michael Barone and Chuck McCutcheon, *The Almanac of American Politics 2014* (Chicago: University of Chicago Press, 2013), 1233.

76 Sean Trende, "In Pennsylvania, the Gerrymander of the Decade?," RealClearPolitics, December 14, 2011, https://www.realclearpolitics.com/articles/2011/12/14/in_pennsylvania_the_gerrymander_of_the_decade_112404.html.

77 Barone and McCutcheon, *Almanac of American Politics 2014,* 369.

78 Barone and McCutcheon, 1566–67.

79 Olga Pierce and Jeff Larson, "How Democrats Fooled California's Redistricting Commission," ProPublica, December 21, 2011, https://www.propublica.org/article/how-democrats-fooled-californias-redistricting-commission.

80 Only partial results for ticket splitting between presidential and House candidates are available in Vital Statistics on Congress prior to 1952. See Table 2–16: https://www.brookings.edu/wp-content/uploads/2019/03/Chpt-2.pdf.

81 Kyle Kondik, "The State of the House," in *The Surge: 2014's Big GOP Win and What It Means For the Next Presidential Election,* ed. Larry J. Sabato, Kyle Kondik, and Geoffrey Skelley (Lanham, MD: Rowman and Littlefield, 2015), 79.

82 Kyle Kondik, "2018 House: The Ground Moving Under Their Feet," *Sabato's Crystal Ball,* February 2, 2017, https://centerforpolitics.org/crystalball/articles/2018-house-the-ground-moving-under-their-feet/.

83 Ronald Brownstein and Leah Askarinam, "House Republicans and Democrats Represent Divergent Americas," *Atlantic,* January 29, 2017, https://www.theatlantic.com/politics/archive/2017/01/house-republicans-racial-education-level/514733/.

84 Jake Sherman and Rachel Bade, "Republicans Sound Alarm Bells on New Jersey Rep. Scott Garrett," *Politico,* September 28, 2016, https://www.politico.com/story/2016/09/scott-garrett-new-jersey-race-congress-help-228838.

85 Robert S. Erikson, "Congressional Elections in Presidential Years: Presidential Coattails and Strategic Voting," *Legislative Studies Quarterly* 41, no. 3 (August 2016): 551–74.

86 Andrew Gelman, "Bob Erikson on the 2018 Midterms," Statistical Modeling, Causal Inference, and Social Science, October 1, 2018, https://statmodeling.stat.columbia.edu/2018/10/01/the-2018-midterms/.

87 Michael J. Malbin, "What the Latest Campaign Finance Filings Can—and Cannot—Tell Us about the Coming Election," Brookings, October 24, 2018, https://www.brookings.edu/blog/fixgov/2018/10/24/what-fec-filings-can-and-cant-tell-us-about-the-election/.

88 Molly Ball, "Why Ossoff Lost," *Atlantic*, June 21, 2017, https://www.theatlantic.com/politics/archive/2017/06/a-crushing-loss-in-georgia-ends-a-losing-season-for-democrats/531072/.

89 "Public Approval of Health Care Bill," RealClearPolitics, https://www.realclearpolitics.com/epolls/other/obama_and_democrats_health_care_plan-1130.html.

90 James A. Stimson, *Tides of Consent*, 2nd ed. (New York: Cambridge University Press, 2015), 70.

91 Nate Cohn, "Democrats Didn't Even Dream of This Pennsylvania Map: How Did It Happen?," *New York Times*, February 21, 2018, https://www.nytimes.com/2018/02/21/upshot/gerrymandering-pennsylvania-democrats-republicans-court.html.

92 Sean Trende, "Redistricting Wars Begin in Illinois," RealClearPolitics, June 7, 2011, https://www.realclearpolitics.com/articles/2011/06/07/redistricting_wars_begin_in_illinois_110116.html.

93 Greg Giroux, "New N.C. Redistricting Boosts Democrats in 2020 Elections," Bloomberg, December 17, 2019, https://about.bgov.com/news/new-nc-redistricting-boosts-democrats-in-2020-elections/.

94 Larry J. Sabato, Kyle Kondik, and J. Miles Coleman, "Final Ratings for the 2020 Election," *Sabato's Crystal Ball*, November 2, 2020, https://centerforpolitics.org/crystalball/articles/21320/.

95 Michael J. Malbin and Brendan Glavin, "Freshman Democrats in House Districts That Trump Carried Are Raising Lots of Money—But So Are Their Challengers," FollowTheMoney.org, February 27, 2020, https://www.followthemoney.org/research/institute-reports/campaign-finance-institute-freshman-democrats-in-house-districts-that-trump-carried-are-raising-lots-of-money-but-so-are-their-challengers.

96 "President Trump Job Approval—Economy," RealClearPolitics, https://www.realclearpolitics.com/epolls/other/president_trump_job_approval_economy-6182.html.

97 Kate Irby, "Republican Flips California Congressional Seat: What Does It Mean for November?," *Sacramento Bee*, May 13, 2020, https://www.sacbee.com/news/politics-government/capitol-alert/article242708631.html.

98 Kyle Kondik, "The Dreaded 269–269 Scenario: An Update," *Sabato's Crystal Ball*, September 16, 2020, https://centerforpolitics.org/crystalball/articles/the-dreaded-269-269-scenario-an-update/.

99 Gary C. Jacobson, "Driven to Extremes: Donald Trump's Extraordinary Impact on the 2020 Elections," *Presidential Studies Quarterly*, June 4, 2021, https://doi.org/10.1111/psq.12724.

100 Patrick Ruffini (@PatrickFuffini), "Three groups shifted in 2020: College whites to Biden, and as they got over 2016, Hispanics and Mormons to Trump. Blacks and Hispanics didn't shift. County-level Asian data isn't great but shifts in Hawaii and Santa Clara County, CA suggest they swung to Trump too," Tweet, December 15, 2020, 10:16 a.m., https://twitter.com/PatrickRuffini /status/1338865479423651840?s=20.

101 Harry Enten, "Trump Made Big In-Roads in Hispanic Areas Across the Nation," CNN, December 12, 2020, https://www.cnn.com/2020/12/12/politics /trump-hispanic-vote/index.html.

102 Jamelle Bouie, "A Simple Theory of Why Trump Did Well," *New York Times,* November 18, 2020, https://www.nytimes.com/2020/11/18/opinion/trump -election-stimulus.html.

103 Jonathan Swan, "Exclusive: Fresh Data Reveal How Trump Made Inroads with Latinos," Axios, April 2, 2021, https://www.axios.com/trump-data-latino -support-49a0foed-b244-4b27-86b3-ee022e21f8c1.html.

104 Mike Memoli, "In Leaked Recording, Biden Says GOP Used 'Defund the Police' to 'Beat the Living Hell' Out of Democrats," NBC News, December 10, 2020, https://www.nbcnews.com/politics/2020-election/leaked -recording-biden-says-gop-used-defund-police-beat-living-n1250757.

105 J. Miles Coleman, "How Mid-Decade Redistrictings Saved the Democratic House Majority," *Sabato's Crystal Ball,* March 18, 2021, https:// centerforpolitics.org/crystalball/articles/how-mid-decade-redistrictings-saved -the-democratic-house-majority/.

106 *Congressional Elections 1946–1996, Congressional Quarterly* (Washington, DC: Congressional Quarterly, 1998), 17–18.

107 Mary Frances McGowan and Leah Askarinam, "Hotline's State Legislative Power Rankings: Democrats Hope to Avenge 2010 Losses," *National Journal,* October 20, 2020, https://www.nationaljournal.com/s/710770/hotlines-state -legislative-power-rankings-democrats-hope-to-avenge-2010-losses.

108 Kyle Kondik, "Redistricting in America, Part One: Gerrymandering Potency Raises the Stakes for the 2020s," *Sabato's Crystal Ball,* July 22, 2021, https:// centerforpolitics.org/crystalball/articles/redistricting-in-america-part -one-gerrymandering-potency-raises-the-stakes-for-the-2020s/.

CONCLUSION

1 Kyle Kondik, "Census Reapportionment: Seat Trade-Offs Likelier to Benefit Republicans," *Sabato's Crystal Ball,* April 26, 2021, https://centerforpolitics. org/crystalball/articles/census-reapportionment-seat-trade-offs-likelier-to -benefit-republicans/.

2 Sarah Ferris, Ally Mutnick, and James Arkin, "Dems Vulnerable to Redistricting Consider Ditching House for Higher Office," *Politico,* March 29, 2021, https:// www.politico.com/news/2021/03/29/house-statewide-redistricting-478211.

BIBLIOGRAPHY

Abramowitz, Alan I. "Moderation in the Pursuit of Victory May Not Help: Evidence from U.S. House Elections, 1978–2018." Paper presented at the Annual Meeting of the American Political Science Association, Marriott Wardman Park Hotel, Washington, DC, August 29–September 2, 2019.

———. "Partisan Redistricting and the 1982 Congressional Elections." *Journal of Politics* 45, no. 3 (August 1983): 767–70.

Abramowitz, Alan I., and Steven Webster. "The Rise of Negative Partisanship and the Nationalization of U.S. Elections in the 21st Century." *Electoral Studies: An International Journal* 41 (March 2016): 12–22.

Ansolabehere, Stephen, and James M. Snyder Jr. *The End of Inequality: One Person, One Vote and the Transformation of American Politics.* New York: W. W. Norton, 2008.

Backstrom, Charles, Samuel Krislov, and Leonard Robins. "Desperately Seeking Standards: The Court's Frustrating Attempts to Limit Political Gerrymandering." *PS: Political Science and Politics* 39, no. 3 (July 2006): 409–15.

Barone, Michael. *Our Country: The Shaping of America from Roosevelt to Reagan.* New York: Free Press, 1990.

Barone, Michael, with Richard E. Cohen. *The Almanac of American Politics 2002.* Washington, DC: National Journal, 2001.

———. *The Almanac of American Politics 2004.* Washington, DC: National Journal, 2003.

———. *The Almanac of American Politics 2006.* Washington, DC: National Journal, 2005.

———. *The Almanac of American Politics 2008.* Washington, DC: National Journal, 2007.

———. *The Almanac of American Politics 2010.* Washington, DC: National Journal, 2009.

Barone, Michael, and Chuck McCutcheon. *The Almanac of American Politics 2012.* Chicago: University of Chicago Press, 2011.

———. *The Almanac of American Politics 2014.* Chicago: University of Chicago Press, 2013.

Barone, Michael, and Grant Ujifusa. *The Almanac of American Politics 1978.* New York: E. P. Dutton, 1977.

————. *The Almanac of American Politics 1980*. New York: E. P. Dutton, 1979.

————. *The Almanac of American Politics 1982*. Washington, DC: Barone, 1981.

————. *The Almanac of American Politics 1984*. Washington, DC: National Journal, 1983.

————. *The Almanac of American Politics 1986*. Washington, DC: National Journal, 1985.

————. *The Almanac of American Politics 1988*. Washington, DC: National Journal, 1987.

————. *The Almanac of American Politics 1990*. Washington, DC: National Journal, 1989.

————. *The Almanac of American Politics 1992*. Washington, DC: National Journal, 1991.

————. *The Almanac of American Politics 1994*. Washington, DC: National Journal, 1993.

————. *The Almanac of American Politics 1996*. Washington, DC: National Journal, 1995.

————. *The Almanac of American Politics 1998*. Washington, DC: National Journal, 1997.

————. *The Almanac of American Politics 2000*. Washington, DC: National Journal, 1999.

Barone, Michael, Grant Ujifusa, and Douglas Matthews. *The Almanac of American Politics 1972*. Boston: Gambit, 1972.

————. *The Almanac of American Politics 1974*. Boston: Gambit, 1973.

————. *The Almanac of American Politics 1976*. New York: E. P. Dutton, 1975.

Bullock, Charles S., III. *Redistricting: The Most Political Activity in America*. 2nd ed. Lanham, MD: Rowman & Littlefield, 2021.

Busch, Andrew E. *Horses in Midstream: U.S. Midterm Elections and Their Consequences, 1894–1998*. Pittsburgh, PA: University of Pittsburgh Press, 1999.

Canon, David T. *Race, Redistricting, and Representation: The Unintended Consequences of Black Majority Districts*. Chicago: University of Chicago Press, 1999.

Cohen, Richard E., with James A. Barnes. *The Almanac of American Politics 2016*. Bethesda, MD: Columbia, 2015.

————. *The Almanac of American Politics 2018*. Bethesda, MD: Columbia, 2017.

Congressional Elections 1946–1996. *Congressional Quarterly*. Washington, DC: Congressional Quarterly, 1998.

Connelly, William F., Jr., and John J. Pitney Jr. *Congress' Permanent Minority? Republicans in the U.S. House*. Lanham, MD: Rowman and Littlefield, 1994.

Cox, Gary W., and Jonathan N. Katz. *Elbridge Gerry's Salamander: The Electoral Consequences of the Reapportionment Revolution*. New York: Cambridge University Press, 2002.

————. "The Reapportionment Revolution and Bias in U.S. Congressional Elections." *American Journal of Political Science* 43, no. 3 (July 1999): 812–41.

Cummings, Milton C., Jr. "Reapportionment in the 1970s: Its Effects on Congress." In *Reapportionment in the 1970s,* edited by Nelson W. Polsby, 209–47. Berkeley: University of California Press, 1971.

Cunningham, Maurice T. *Maximization, Whatever the Cost: Race, Redistricting, and the Department of Justice.* Westport, CT: Praeger, 2001.

Curry, James M., and Frances E. Lee. *The Limits of Party: Congress and Lawmaking in a Polarized Era.* Chicago: University of Chicago Press, 2020.

Dimock, Michael A., and Gary C. Jacobson. "Checks and Choices: The House Bank Scandal's Impact on Voters in 1992." *Journal of Politics* 57, no. 4 (November 1995): 1143–59.

Dow, Jay K. *Electing the House: The Adoption and Performance of the US Single-Member District Electoral System.* Lawrence: University Press of Kansas, 2017.

Elliott, Ward. "Prometheus, Proteus, Pandora, and Procrustes Unbound: The Political Consequences of Reapportionment." *University of Chicago Law Review* 37, no. 3 (Spring 1970): 474–92.

Engstrom, Erik J. *Partisan Gerrymandering and the Construction of American Democracy.* Ann Arbor: University of Michigan Press, 2013.

Erikson, Robert S. "Congressional Elections in Presidential Years: Presidential Coattails and Strategic Voting." *Legislative Studies Quarterly* 41, no. 3 (August 2016): 551–74.

———. "Malapportionment, Gerrymandering, and Party Fortunes in Congressional Elections." *American Political Science Review* 66, no. 4 (December 1972): 1234–45.

———. "Why the Democrats Lose Presidential Elections: Toward a Theory of Optimal Loss." *PS: Political Science and Politics* 22, no. 1 (March 1989): 30–35.

Gelman, Andrew, and Gary King. "Enhancing Democracy through Legislative Redistricting." *American Political Science Review* 88, no. 3 (September 1994): 541–59.

Glazer, Amihai, Bernard Grofman, and Marc Robbins. "Partisan and Incumbency Effects of 1970s Congressional Redistricting." *American Journal of Political Science* 31, no. 3 (August 1987): 680–707.

Griffith, Elmer C. *The Rise and Development of the Gerrymander.* Chicago: Scott, Foresman, 1907.

Grofman, Bernard, and Thomas L. Brunell. "The Art of the Dummymander: The Impact of Recent Redistrictings on the Partisan Makeup of Southern House Seats." In *Redistricting in the New Millennium,* edited by Peter F. Galderisi, 183–99. Lanham, MD: Lexington, 2005.

Grose, Christian R. *Congress in Black and White: Race and Representation in Washington and at Home.* New York: Cambridge University Press, 2011.

Hacker, Andrew. *Congressional Districting: The Issue of Equal Representation.* Washington, DC: Brookings Institution, 1963.

Harris, Douglas B. "Legislative Parties and Leadership Choice: Confrontation or Accommodation in the 1989 Gingrich-Madigan Whip Race." *American Politics Research* 34, no. 2 (March 2006): 189–222.

Harris, John F. *The Survivor: Bill Clinton in the White House.* New York: Random House, 2006.

Hopkins, David A. *Red Fighting Blue: How Geography and Electoral Rules Polarize American Politics.* New York: Cambridge University Press, 2017.

Hunter, Thomas Rogers. "The First Gerrymander? Patrick Henry, James Madison, James Monroe, and Virginia's 1788 Congressional Districting." *Early American Studies: An Interdisciplinary Journal* 9, no. 3 (Fall 2011): 781–820.

Issacharoff, Samuel. "Gerrymandering and Political Cartels." *Harvard Law Review* 116, no. 2 (December 2002): 593–648.

Jacobson, Gary C. "Driven to Extremes: Donald Trump's Extraordinary Impact on the 2020 Elections." *Presidential Studies Quarterly,* June 4, 2021. https://doi.org/10.1111/psq.12724.

———. *The Electoral Origins of Divided Government: Competition in U.S. House Elections, 1946–1988.* Boulder, CO: Westview, 1990.

———. "Extreme Referendum: Donald Trump and the 2018 Midterm Elections." *Political Science Quarterly* 134, no. 1 (Spring 2019): 9–38.

———. "It's Nothing Personal: The Decline of the Incumbency Advantage in US House Elections." *Journal of Politics* 77, no. 3 (July 2015): 861–73.

Jacobson, Gary C., and Jamie L. Carson. *The Politics of Congressional Elections.* 10th ed. Lanham, MD: Rowman and Littlefield, 2020.

Kondik, Kyle. "House 2016: The Republicans Endure." In *Trumped: The 2016 Election That Broke All the Rules,* edited by Larry J. Sabato, Kyle Kondik, and Geoffrey Skelley, 70–82. Lanham, MD: Rowman and Littlefield, 2017.

———. "The House: A Blue Wave Reduced to a Blue Trickle." In *A Return to Normalcy? The 2020 Election That (Almost) Broke America,* edited by Larry J. Sabato, Kyle Kondik, and J. Miles Coleman, 101–13. Lanham, MD: Rowman and Littlefield, 2021.

———. "The House: Where the Blue Wave Hit the Hardest." In *The Blue Wave: The 2018 Midterms and What They Mean for the 2020 Elections,* edited by Larry J. Sabato and Kyle Kondik, 98–114. Lanham, MD: Rowman and Littlefield, 2019.

———. "Republicans Hold the Line: 2012's National House Contest." In *Barack Obama and the New America,* edited by Larry J. Sabato, 143–51. Lanham, MD: Rowman and Littlefield, 2013.

———. "The State of the House." In *The Surge: 2014's Big GOP Win and What It Means For the Next Presidential Election,* edited by Larry J. Sabato, Kyle Kondik, and Geoffrey Skelley, 73–85. Lanham, MD: Rowman and Littlefield, 2015.

Kornacki, Steve. *The Red and the Blue: The 1990s and the Birth of Political Tribalism.* New York: HarperCollins, 2018.

Lee, Frances E. *Insecure Majorities: Congress and the Perpetual Campaign.* Chicago: University of Chicago Press, 2016.

Lublin, David. *The Paradox of Representation: Racial Gerrymandering and Minority Interests in Congress.* Princeton, NJ: Princeton University Press, 1997.

———. *The Republican South: Democratization and Partisan Change.* Princeton, NJ: Princeton University Press, 2004.

Lyons, Michael, and Peter F. Galderisi. "Incumbency, Reapportionment, and U.S. House Redistricting." *Political Research Quarterly* 48, no. 4 (December 1995): 857–71.

Mann, Thomas E. "Is the House of Representatives Unresponsive to Political Change?" In *Elections American Style,* edited by A. James Reichley, 261–82. Washington, DC: Brookings Institution, 1987.

———. "Redistricting Reform: What Is Desirable? Possible?" In *Party Lines: Competition, Partisanship, and Congressional Redistricting,* edited by Thomas E. Mann and Bruce E. Cain, 92–114. Washington, DC: Brookings Institution, 2005.

Martis, Kenneth C. *The Historical Atlas of United States Congressional Districts, 1789–1983.* New York: Free Press, 1982.

Mayhew, David R. "Congressional Representation: Theory and Practice in Drawing the Districts." In *Reapportionment in the 1970s,* edited by Nelson W. Polsby, 249–90. Berkeley: University of California Press, 1971.

McGann, Anthony J., Charles Anthony Smith, Michael Latner, and Alex Keena. *Gerrymandering in America: The House of Representatives, the Supreme Court, and the Future of Popular Sovereignty.* New York: Cambridge University Press, 2016.

McKee, Seth C. *Republican Ascendancy in Southern U.S. House Elections.* Boulder, CO: Westview, 2010.

Monmonier, Mark. *Bushmanders and Bullwinkles: How Politicians Manipulate Electronic Maps and Census Data to Win Elections.* Chicago: University of Chicago Press, 2001.

Niemi, Richard G., and Alan I. Abramowitz. "Partisan Redistricting and the 1992 Congressional Elections." *Journal of Politics* 56, no. 3 (August 1994): 811–17.

Nokken, Timothy P., and Keith T. Poole. "Congressional Party Defection in American History." *Legislative Studies Quarterly* 29, no. 4 (November 2004): 545–68.

Persily, Nathaniel, Thad Kousser, and Patrick Egan. "The Complicated Impact of One Person, One Vote on Political Competition and Representation." *North Carolina Law Review* 80, no. 4 (2002): 1299–1352.

Rae, Nicol C. *The Decline and Fall of the Liberal Republicans from 1952 to the Present.* New York: Oxford University Press, 1989.

———. *Southern Democrats.* New York: Oxford University Press, 1994.

Remini, Robert V. *The House: The History of the House of Representatives.* Washington, DC: Smithsonian Books, 2007.

Rodden, Jonathan A. *Why Cities Lose: The Deep Roots of the Urban-Rural Political Divide.* New York: Basic Books, 2019.

Rosenfeld, Sam. *The Polarizers: Postwar Architects of Our Partisan Era.* Chicago: University of Chicago Press, 2018.

Rush, Mark E. *Does Redistricting Make a Difference? Partisan Representation and Electoral Behavior.* Baltimore: Johns Hopkins University Press, 1993.

Sabato, Larry J. "The George W. Bush Midterm." In *Midterm Madness: The Elections of 2002,* edited by Larry J. Sabato, 1–34. Lanham, MD: Rowman and Littlefield, 2003.

Scammon, Richard M. *America Votes 6 (1964): A Handbook of Contemporary Voting Statistics.* Washington, DC: Congressional Quarterly, 1966.

———. *America Votes 7 (1966): A Handbook of Contemporary Voting Statistics.* Washington, DC: Congressional Quarterly, 1968.

———. *America Votes 8 (1968): A Handbook of Contemporary Voting Statistics.* Washington, DC: Congressional Quarterly, 1967.

Seabrook, Nicholas R. *Drawing the Lines: Constraints on Partisan Gerrymandering in U.S. Politics.* Ithaca, NY: Cornell University Press, 2017.

Shelley, Mark C., II. *The Permanent Majority: The Conservative Coalition in the United States Congress.* Tuscaloosa: University of Alabama Press, 1983.

Sickels, Robert J. "Dragons, Bacon Strips and Dumbbells—Who's Afraid of Reapportionment?" *Yale Law Journal* 75, no. 8 (July 1966): 1300–1308.

Smith, David R., and Thomas L. Brunell. "Special Elections to the U.S. House of Representatives: A General Election Barometer?" *Legislative Studies Quarterly* 35, no. 2 (May 2010): 283–97.

Smith, J. Douglas. *On Democracy's Doorstep: The Inside Story of How the Supreme Court Brought "One Person, One Vote" to the United States.* New York: Hill and Wang, 2014.

Stephanopoulos, Nicholas O., and Eric M. McGhee. "Partisan Gerrymandering and the Efficiency Gap." *University of Chicago Law Review* 82, no. 2 (March 2015): 831–900.

Stimson, James A. *Tides of Consent,* 2nd ed. New York: Cambridge University Press, 2015.

Stonecash, Jeffrey M. *Interpreting Congressional Elections: The Curious Case of the Incumbency Effect.* New York: Routledge, 2018.

Tomasky, Michael. *Bill Clinton.* New York: Times, 2017.

Trende, Sean. *The Lost Majority: Why the Future of Government Is Up for Grabs—and Who Will Take It.* New York: Palgrave Macmillan, 2012.

Tufte, Edward R. "The Relationship between Seats and Votes in Two-Party Systems." *American Political Science Review* 67, no. 2 (June 1973): 540–54.

Voss, D. Stephen, and David Lublin. "Black Incumbents, White Districts: An Appraisal of the 1996 Congressional Elections." *American Politics Research* 29, no. 2 (March 2001): 141–82.

Wasserman, David. "The 2006 House Midterm Maelstrom." In *The Sixth Year Itch: The Rise and Fall of the George W. Bush Presidency,* edited by Larry J. Sabato, 97–133. New York: Pearson Longman, 2008.

Zelizer, Julian E. *Burning Down the House: Newt Gingrich, the Fall of a Speaker, and the Rise of the New Republican Party.* New York: Penguin Press, 2020.

INDEX

Abbitt, Watkins, 33
Abramowitz, Alan I., 43, 53, 74–75
Abscam, 51
Abzug, Bella, 49
Affordable Care Act, 3–4, 94, 105–6
Agnew, Spiro, 33
Alabama, 20–21, 24, 28, 30, 66, 77; as part of Greater South, 7; redistricting in, 20, 61, 84–85; AL-2, 92; AL-6, 61
Alaska, 29; as part of Interior West, 7
Albuquerque, NM, 92
Almanac of American Politics, 7, 50, 60–61, 63, 78, 89
Altmire, Jason, 96–97
American National Election Studies, 74
Annapolis, MD, 31
Anne Arundel County, MD, 31
Apple, R. W., Jr., 64
Arizona, 20, 30, 65, 89, 113, 117; as part of Interior West, 7; redistricting in, 56, 98; AZ-1, 86; AZ-3, 54
Arkansas, 28, 60; as part of Greater South, 7; redistricting in, 24; AR-3, 24, 36; AR-4, 99
Armey, Dick, 56–57
Arrington, Theodore S., 7, 69–70, 121
Askarinam, Leah, 102
Aspinall, Wayne, 31–32
Atkinson, Eugene, 54
Atlanta, GA, 24, 32, 49, 58, 61, 105, 108, 112, 116
Axne, Cindy, 116

Bachus, Spencer, 61
Bacon, Don, 116
Baker v. Carr, xiii, 13
Baldwin, Tammy, 81
Ball, Molly, 105
Baltimore, MD, 31, 85
Barone, Michael, 50, 53, 78, 89
Barr, Andy, 99
Barrow, John, 91, 100
Bartlett, Roscoe, 99

Barton, Joe, 54
Bass, Charlie, 95
Baton Rouge, LA, 36
Belcher, Page, 31
Bendavid, Naftali, 89
Bennett, Charles, 61
Beutler, Jamie Herrera, 95
Biden, Joe, 54, 74–75, 111–19
Bishop, Dan, 109
Blagojevich, Rod, 79, 89
Boehner, John, 101
Bonilla, Henry, 91
Bouie, Jamelle, 118
Brademas, John, 51
Brat, Dave, 101
Brennan Center for Justice, 71
Brindisi, Anthony, 115
Brooks, Jack, 78
Broward County, FL, 24
Brown, Corrine, 61
Brown, Jerry, 56
Brownstein, Ron, 102
Brown-Waite, Ginny, 85
Brunell, Thomas, 34, 72
Bullock, Charles S., III, 13
Burton, Philip, 53, 56, 60
Burton, Sala, 56
Busch, Andrew E., 21, 34, 45, 48, 55
Bush, George H. W., 5, 25–26, 40, 44, 49, 58–61, 63, 73, 77, 84, 119, 127
Bush, George W., 49, 68, 82–84, 86–89, 91–92, 118
Bustos, Cheri, 115–16

Cabell, Earle, 31
California, 28, 30, 48, 60, 65, 82, 100, 110, 113, 116–17, 119; as part of West Coast, 8; redistricting in, 14, 34, 53, 56, 85, 98–99; CA-5, 53; CA-8, 91; CA-11, 85; CA-21, 51; CA-25, 113, 116; CA-31, 99–100; CA-38, 56; CA-39, 117; CA-48, 117

Hultgren, Randy, 108
Humphrey, Hubert, 27–28
Hurd, Will, 111
Hurricane Katrina, 88
Hyde, Henry, 30

Idaho, as part of Interior West, 7
Illinois, 35, 38, 52–53, 60, 79, 89, 92; as part of
    Midwest, 8; redistricting in, 30, 54, 99, 108;
    IL-3, 112; IL-5, 79, 89; IL-6, 108; IL-10, 51,
    102; IL-12, 101, 108; IL-13, 108; IL-14, 75, 92,
    108, 115; IL-15, 47; IL-17, 115; IL-18, 52
Indiana, 35, 47, 57–59, 65, 89; as part of Mid-
    west, 8; redistricting in, 30–31, 53, 76; IN-2,
    99; IN-3, 51; IN-4, 47; IN-5, 112, 116; IN-8,
    53, 57–58; IN-9, 82; IN-11, 31
Indianapolis, IN, 31, 112
Inhofe, James, 58
Inslee, Jay, 81
Interior West, 29, 37, 46, 53, 65, 77–78, 90, 95,
    120, 124–25, 127; regional definition of, 7
Iowa, 19, 23, 30, 112; as part of Midwest, 8; IA-
    1, 101, 115; IA-2, 112, 115; IA-3, 116; IA-4, 112
Iran-Contra, 58
Iraq War, 68, 84, 88, 91, 124
Ireland, Andy, 54
Iron Range, MN, 94
Israel, Steve, 82
Issacharoff, Samuel, 70–71

Jacksonville, FL, 61
Jacobs, Andrew, Jr., 31
Jacobson, Gary C., 7, 43, 45, 55, 62, 75, 114
James, Craig, 58
Jenrette, John, 51
Jim Crow laws, 16, 32
Johnson, Lyndon B., 16–18, 22–23, 26, 31, 38,
    41, 59, 62, 94
Jones, James, 31, 58
Jordan, Barbara, 32

Kansas, as part of Interior West, 7; KS-2, 112
Kasich, John, 54
Katko, John, 116
Katz, Jonathan N., 15
Keena, Alex, 73–74
Keith, Hastings, 31
Kelly, Richard, 36
Kemp, Jack, 30, 48
Kennedy, Anthony, 14
Kennedy, John F., 22, 59, 119
Kennedy, Mark, 83
Kennedy, Robert, 26

Kent County, MI, 47
Kentucky, 59, 64; as part of Greater South,
    7–8; KY-3, 78, 81; KY-6, 88, 99
Kerry, John, 87–88, 90–91
Kilroy, Mary Jo, 92
Kim, Andy, 116
Kim, Young, 117
Kind, Ron, 115
King, Gary, 72
King, Martin Luther, Jr., 26
King, Steve, 112
Klink, Ron, 82
Klug, Scott, 81
Koch, Ed, 27, 49
Kornacki, Steve, 63
Kostmayer, Peter, 54
Kousser, Thad, 14
Kucinich, Dennis, 79

LaCaze, Jeff, 36
Lake Michigan, 51
Lamb, Conor, 106–7, 109, 115
Lampson, Nick, 78
Lansing, MI, 20
Latner, Michael, 73–74
Laughlin, Greg, 77
Lazio, Rick, 82
Lee, Frances, 4, 43, 52
Lehigh Valley, PA, 106
Lewinsky, Monica, 79–80
Lewis, John, 58
Li, Michael, 71
Lindsay, John, 27
Lipinski, Dan, 112
Lott, Trent, 32
Louisiana, 20, 28, 32, 36, 59, 65; as part of
    Greater South, 7; redistricting in, 71, 78;
    LA-3, 32, 77; LA-5, 78; LA-6, 36
Louisville, KY, 78, 81
Lublin, David, 16, 42–43, 45, 71
Luken, Tom, 47

Macomb County, MI, 20
Madigan, Edward, 30, 52
Madison, James, 11
Madison, WI, 81
Maine, as part of Northeast, 8; redistricting in,
    56; ME-2, 101, 109, 116
Major League Baseball, 28
malapportionment, 12–15, 19–20; definition
    of, 10
Malbin, Michael, 104, 112
Maloney, James, 81

Manhattan, NY, 27, 29, 49
Mann, Thomas, 45, 62, 72
Margolies-Mezvinsky, Marjorie, 63, 81
Marshall, Jim, 91
Maryland, as part of Northeast, 8; redistricting
in, 24–25, 31, 57, 85, 99; MD-2, 85; MD-4,
31; MD-6, 99; MD-8, 85
Mason-Dixon line, 24
Massachusetts, 26, 79, 95, 117; as part of North-
east, 8; redistricting in, 11, 31; MA-12, 31
Matheson, Jim, 83, 100
Mayhew, David, 14
McAdams, Ben, 115
McBath, Lucy, 108–9
McCain, John, 91, 93–94
McCloskey, Frank, 53, 57
McCready, Dan, 109
McEachin, Don, 102
McGann, Anthony J., 73–74
McGhee, Eric, 70, 76
McGovern, George, 30
McIntyre, Mike, 96, 100
McIntyre, Richard, 57
McKay, Gunn, 51
McKee, Seth, 16
McMillan, John, 33
McNerney, Jerry, 85
Meehan, Pat, 106–7
Memphis, TN, 25
Miami-Dade County, FL, 58, 117
Michel, Bob, 52
Michigan, 11, 35, 60, 95, 108; as part of Mid-
west, 8; redistricting in, 19–20, 23, 84–85,
97; MI-5, 33, 35, 47; MI-6, 54; MI-8, 108,
116; MI-11, 108; MI-12, 19; MI-18, 19
midterm elections: desire for balance, 103–4;
falling performance of presidential candi-
dates in, 72; House majorities more fre-
quently lost in, 45; presidential party gains
in, 79–80, 88; propensity for presidential
party losses, 5, 21–22
Midwest, 2, 19, 25, 30, 37, 46, 49–50, 53, 65,
77, 85, 90, 95, 97, 120, 124–25, 127; regional
definition of, 8
Mikva, Abner, 51
Minge, David, 83
Minish, Joseph, 57
Minneapolis/St. Paul (Twin Cities), MN, 51,
104, 118
Minnesota, 29, 83, 94, 104, 115; as part of
Midwest, 8; redistricting in, 54; MN-1, 107;
MN-2, 83, 115; MN-3, 104, 115; MN-6, 51;
MN-7, 29, 115; MN-8, 94, 107

Mississippi, 20–21, 24, 28, 32, 58, 66, 85; as
part of Greater South, 7; MS-1, 92; MS-4,
77, 94
Missouri, 83; as part of Midwest, 8; MO-1, 112;
MO-4, 94; MO-6, 83
Mizell, Wilmer, 28
Mondale, Walter, 49
Monroe, James, 11
Montana, as part of Interior West, 7; redis-
tricting in, 56; MT-AL, 78
Montgomery County, MD, 24
Moore, W. Henson, III, 36
Morella, Constance, 85
Morris, Dick, 1
Mosher, Charles, 47
Murphy, John, 51
Murtha, John, 33

National Republican Congressional Commit-
tee, 103
Nebraska, 23, 116; as part of Interior West, 7;
NE-2, 100, 103, 116
Nevada, as part of Interior West, 7; NV-3, 86
New Deal, 2, 17–18, 77
New England, 90, 92, 99, 109
New Hampshire, 89–90, 95, 99; as part of
Northeast, 8; NH-1, 103; NH-2, 95
New Jersey, 19, 103; as part of Northeast, 8;
redistricting in, 28, 57, 98; NJ-2, 113; NJ-3,
116; NJ-4, 51; NJ-5, 103; NJ-11, 57; NJ-12, 81
New Mexico, as part of Interior West, 7; redis-
tricting in, 27; NM-1, 90; NM-2, 115
New Orleans, LA, 32, 88
New York, 19, 30, 35, 38, 49, 53, 60, 76, 86, 89,
92, 95; as part of Northeast, 8; redistricting
in, 14, 27, 29, 35, 54; NY-2, 82; NY-9, 49;
NY-11, 101, 115; NY-12, 27; NY-16, 112; NY-
17, 51; NY-18, 29, 49; NY-22, 115; NY-24,
116; NY-38, 48
New York City, 27, 35, 49, 84
New York Times, 10, 29, 48, 57, 64, 118
Ney, Bob, 90
Nixon, Richard M., 15, 21, 24, 27–30, 33–34,
38, 46, 59, 119
Nokken, Timothy P., 25
Nolan, Rick, 51
North Carolina, 36, 58, 64, 89, 100, 109, 116,
122, 126, 128; as part of Greater South, 7;
redistricting in, 28, 57, 74, 76, 96, 102, 111,
119; NC-2, 79, 111; NC-4, 79; NC-5, 28;
NC-6, 111; NC-7, 96, 100; NC-9, 109; NC-
11, 89; NC-12, 70–71
North Dakota, 23, 30; as part of Interior West, 7

About the Author

Kyle Kondik is managing editor of *Sabato's Crystal Ball*, a nonpartisan political newsletter on campaigns and elections produced by the University of Virginia Center for Politics. He analyzes US House elections as well as those for president, Senate, and governor.

He is also the center's communications director and manages the center's Washington, DC, office. He is the author of *The Bellwether* (2016, Ohio University Press), a history of presidential elections in Ohio, and has been an editor of and contributor to several other books on American campaigns and elections. He holds a master's degree in government from Johns Hopkins University and a bachelor's degree in journalism from Ohio University.

He and his wife, Lottie Walker, live in Washington, DC, along with their young son, Albert.